Ethics in Business

Ethics in Business

Concept, Cases and Context

Ananda Das Gupta

RAWAT PUBLICATIONS
Jaipur and New Delhi

ISBN 81-7033-855-7

Published by
Prem Rawat for **Rawat Publications**
Satyam Apts., Sector 3, Jawahar Nagar, Jaipur 302 004 (India)
Phone: 0141 265 1748 / 7006 Fax: 0141 265 1748
E-mail: info@rawatbooks.com
Website: www.rawatbooks.com

Delhi Office
4858/24, Ansari Road, Daryaganj, New Delhi 110 002
Phone: 011 23263290

Typeset by Rawat Computers, Jaipur
Printed at Chaman Enterprises, New Delhi

Contents

Preface

I

Corporate responsibility is a vital issue in contemporary business climate. Much of its currency comes from the scale and influence of the present-day corporate world. Some business houses are bigger than many nation-states. Their domain and economic imperialism is worldwide. Nevertheless, business houses are subject to constant and intense scrutiny and surveillance by the state and the society in which they function. It is well established that their freedom to operate is not a licence to abuse.

Of course, profit has to be the primary concern of any business: without profit, it is impossible to carry out any other activity for the welfare of the society at large. However, there are two overriding criteria, which assume significance in this context. While profit may be the overall objective, the methods employed to achieve profit have to be above board, they must be ethical and moral. Secondly, having achieved profit, the company must look around for ways and means by which it can return to the society some endowments for the welfare of everyone. The *summum bonum* of any enterprise is the lofty and noble objectives it seeks to serve in and for the society, in which it subsists.

The emerging values of humanism and humanisation, coupled with the burgeoning focus on creativity, the autonomy, which people are acquiring progressively, and the focus of supply and demand, have forced CEOs to acknowledge 'people power'.

Moreover, people's expectations are fast changing and they cannot be taken for granted. They have the motivation to work and are to be treated different from other resources. As such, the conventional approach of personnel management to people treating them as a resource, as unnecessary evils who can only be motivated through fear, punishment, money or comfort, has undergone a sea-change.

"Knowledge is the only meaningful resource today," said Peter F. Drucker. An organisation is run through many resources like material, money, machines, land, building, capital, etc., and access to them is no longer limited. As access to people – the most vital resource – is limited, they dictate the market forces of supply and demand, as they are knowledge workers. People being the most fragile, sensitive resources are also costly to maintain. An expenditure on them is an investment, for, this resource accelerates in values whereas the other resources depreciate over a period of time. Hence, the need to give greater importance to them.

Being aware of their importance to the corporates in India, which is emerging as a mighty industrial order of the East, the new entrants to organisations look upon employment as an opportunity to test their knowledge and apply the same to the work situation. Today's professionals have been much more demanding than their predecessors. These professionals have the potential to determine their own performance. The emerging trends of the new paradigm of business involving open market operations in the labour market, viz., free competition, total quality movement, mergers as well as alliances of Indian companies with known cash-rich MNCs, have prompted obliging CEOs to give special importance to people.

Meeting the challenges of the business and trade with opening up of the Indian economy to the world and acquiring a higher share of the market is no longer an easy task. Corporates in the search for developing the cutting edge have experienced that it is the knowledge worker who has to be developed, trained and retained. The earlier view that the cost of labour in the country being comparatively low, cheap labour is an asset for Indian companies, no longer holds good. Today, skilled and trained labour is a costly factor of production. Indian companies need knowledge workers, who can bring both knowledge and expertise into the business. The three strengths needed today for corporates to be effective – one, being innovative in market, two, developing originality of service, and three, a deep understanding of needs of the customer – can be acquired through knowledge and that is the people.

We are moving towards a knowledge-based society. Management of the knowledge worker is therefore crucial. Organisations with vision to be world class entrepreneurs have to nurture knowledge workers. This is absolutely necessary for two reasons, namely, that the human resource has the potential to create competitive edge for the organisation but it is a scarce resource. Further, significance is being attached to people since today it is the only resource which corporates are unable to transfer freely across national boundaries, which is a matter of necessity in today's business. Therefore, those corporates who operate as boundaryless information, technology and capital, is an indication of how to do away with the old concepts of business at home. Thus, these corporates are able to train and develop people of one nation to take up positions in the newly started operations anywhere in the world. Success of such boundaryless corporates entirely depends upon the availability of local top class intellectual capital which has accentuated the value of people and as such acquisition of the right talent has turned out to be crucial.

Human beings, being the makers of knowledge juggernaut, due to their expert knowledge, will be able to deal with the diverse nature of functions of the entire corporate activities, leading to customer satisfaction.

Earlier, this role was played by the corporate's chief strategist, i.e., the CEO and his top management team. This is the changing role of the knowledge worker. Since we know that contemporary CEO's prime concern of late is customer (both internal and external) satisfaction, satisfying customer needs is an act, which involves leveraging knowledge of the organisation's potential to provide satisfaction to the customer. This is to be done through the people, who are the fountainhead of knowledge.

Increasing importance of people therefore is due to the ever-increasing demands of the customers. All corporate strengths depend upon the people. Thus, it is the people who have the knowledge and can develop the competitive edge of any organisation. People thus are the centre piece of all organisational activities.

People are also being valued more since they are the fountainhead of all winning concepts. New products are created by intensive and extensive planned research and development. Developing successful products is the result of the knowledge deployed as a core competence of the corporate. In manufacturing operations too, the role of people is most vital due to the use of high precision, high-tech equipment and machinery in shops. Today, induction of CNC/NC machines and automation has revolutionised the industry and led to reduction in use of manpower. Individuals are to operate as part of an effective team and their contribution is crucial to the performance of the entire group/section. As such, success of a manufacturing organisation will depend not merely on its use of updated sophisticated technology but also what may be called the intrinsic way the people use the technology optimally and purposefully.

In the field of marketing, organisations are covering the clone products with layers of unique service in an effort to introduce novel and attractive types of customer satisfaction. But, the 'quality of the service' component, which is crucial for generating customer value, is contingent upon the individual person's ability to deliver the same. Hence, the need for a knowledge worker, who has the capability to perform in the present-day situation, is underlined. The organisation's focus on customer satisfaction is further reinforced by the marketing professionals' emphasis on developing a healthy relationship between the buyer and the organisation by offering different services. While service has progressively become the hallmark in the global economy, people are the more being looked upon as the most vital instrument for providing satisfaction to the customer.

II

The *New Organizational Order* can only succeed by being open to the harmonious and conflictual redistribution of information and energy around the pattern as a whole. For the pattern to maintain its coherence and integrity, care must be taken to ensure the emergence of a complement to every portion of the pattern; such counter-patterns counteract and absorb each other's excesses and energise each other's evolution.

The *New Organizational Order* cannot ultimately depend upon a single pattern to redistribute energies in response to present circumstances. Different patterns need to emerge according to the diversity to be interrelated and in response to the continuing pressures of human and social development. Familiarity with the range of patterning possibilities, and how their emergence may be facilitated, is an important factor in making this alternatives viable.

The *New Organizational Order* will prove most significant when the transition between patterns can itself be made in harmony with a pattern of a yet higher order.

Acknowledgement

While working on my other book entitled, *Human Values in Management*, which has recently been published by Ashgate Publishing Limited, Hampshire, England, I have had the opportunity of interacting with many eminent scholars, drawing from different parts of the world, in the fields of business ethics and human values in management and this book is an outcome of the insights which I received from them.

I specially thank my friend Dr. Bengt Gustavsson of Swedish Business School in Stockholm University for his valuable comments that he made while going through the initial drafts.

I also thank Prof. S. K. Chakraborty for having suggested that instead of the term 'business ethics', we should coin the term as 'ethics in business'.

In this process, I thank Dr. Subhash Sharma, Director, Indian Institute of Plantation Management, Bangalore, for his encouragement and the interest he has shown in my endeavour. He also put forward cogent and valuable comments and suggestions towards improving the general idea of the book.

I should not forget the help and support being provided by my wife Aruna Das Gupta, who herself is on the threshold of completing her dissertation in the very fascinating area of the impact of Vivekananda's thoughts on modern corporate world towards reaching a sacro-civic world. I also take the opportunity of thanking my daughter Debarati for being skeptical about the prospect of the book.

In the process of writing this book, Mr. Shaji Kurien, Programme Associate of our Institute has helped me in all possible directions. I am thankful to him.

Lastly, it will not be appropriate if I forget to mention the name of Mr. Pranit Rawat, who, first of all, has taken keen interest in publishing this book under their reputed and established banner. I thank his endeavour and scholarly mind.

1

Foundation of the Indian Moral System

The Indian moral system contains within it both social ethics and individual ethics. The whole of the Indian moral system proceeds on the assumption that as a human being, every man has to discharge two types of moral obligations – one related to the other member of society and the other related to one's own self. Under the former are included such virtues or duties as *ahimsa* (non-violence), *dana* (charity), *daya* (compassion), *paropakara* (help or service to others), *asana, prnayama* and such other methods of *cittasuddi,* etc. The idea here is that morality is the inculcation and practice of characteristic human virtues as against animal inclinations. The question of the inculcation or practice of such human virtues or duties arises not only in relation to members of society, but in relation to oneself also by virtue of one being a man, and not an animal.

The Indian outlook is spiritual and the Indian moral system is oriented towards a spiritual goal. The spiritual goal is generally known as *moksha* and morality in any of its forms is a means to that goal. So, morality in India is thoroughly spiritualistic. There is a materialist system of thought also in the Indian tradition, which neither believes in the spiritual foundation of the world nor in spiritual goals. But, the tone of the system is so meagre in the overall spiritualistic atmosphere, that it has hardly any impact on the Indian moral system.

The Indian moral system has a metaphysical basis. In the West, ethics is autonomous and it does not need to have a metaphysical or religious foundation. It is a social affair and, therefore, the ought-questions of morality are to be decided simply on social and rational considerations. It does not need to have any transcendental basis. Moreover, metaphysics purports to deal with factual (although of a fundamental nature) questions and purely factual considerations can never become a foundation for deciding ought-questions. For, from mere "is", there is non-passage to "ought". If, however, we make such a passage, we become victim of a fallacy popularly known as "naturalistic fallacy". The two distinguishable features of the Indian concept of morality are as follows: (1) authority has the basis for deciding what is moral and what is immoral, and (2) morality refers not only to social obligations, but also to obligations related to one's own self.

Indian ethics have been more perceptive than speculative or critical. Indian thinkers have always adopted a practical outlook and consequently they have never separated theoretical thinking from their practical consequences. This is obvious in Indian philosophical thinking, conspicuously marked, as it is, by the practical concern of liberating people from the ocean of worldly misery. Even in logical thinking, this concern may be seen in the Indian logician's refusal to make a sharp distinction between formal and material truth or between deduction and induction. This concern finds articulation in Indian ethics, which is by and large perceptive, prescriptive or normative. In other words, the primary concern of Indian ethics has been to prescribe norms for a morally elevated life in both its personal and social aspects.

Moreover, the Indian moral system is out and out humanistic. To many western scholars, this characteristic may sound just the opposite of what they have so far thought to be the actual position. Many western thinkers dealing with the ethical aspect of Indian thought have opined that room for humanistic ethics in Indian thought is unlikely, because it is basically other worldly and life-negating in its approach. Such an impression about Indian thought betrays one's utter ignorance about its true nature and spirit. The *Advaita Vedanta* does not deny the reality of this world outright. On the contrary, it fully firms the reality of the world from the practical standpoint. And from this standpoint, all ordinary human relationships are fully real, so there is full-fledged scope for a humanistic ethics. Even from the real standpoint, or what may even be called the transcendental standpoint, *Samakara* does not so much deny the reality of this world as it insists on re-interpreting it. According to him, what is to be realised from the real standpoint is not that the world is a complete void, but that it fully spiritual and devoid of multiplicity. The multiplicity and materiality are illusions. What is real is the spiritual unity. And what can be a more solid basis for humanistic ethics, rather for universalistic ethics, than this kind of realisation that the apparent multiplicity of the world is sheer illusion and what is real is a basic spiritual unity? This will be still clearer if we try to see to some extent what humanism actually means and implies.

Modern Indian thinkers such as Vivekananda, Tagore and Gandhi have sought to make morality a direct means to *moksha*. They presented such a conception of *moksha* that even social morality by itself becomes directly relevant for the attainment of *moksha*. *Moksha* for them is nothing other than what Tagore specifically calls realising oneself into others and others into oneself, or else realising, the universal self within the individual self. Such a realisation, they point out, perhaps rightly, is possible only by cultivating the social virtues of compassion, love, brotherhood, etc. Morality becomes a path of direct relevance for the attainment of the highest ideal of life.

The rightness and wrongness of an action is determined with reference to its conduciveness or un-conduciveness to pre-accepted, non-moral goals. The theory of ethics based on answers of this type is known as teleological theory. The other type does not refer to any ulterior non-moral end or goal.

According to peledogial theory, an action is right or wrong by virtue of its own merit or demerit and not in terms of the goal that it leads to or does not lead to. The theory of ethics based on answers of this kind is known as deontological theory.

Deontological theories deny what teleological theories affirm. They deny that the right, the obligatory and the morally good are wholly, whether directly or indirectly, a function of what is non-morally good. They assert that there are other considerations that may make an action or rule right or obligatory besides the goodness or badness of its consequences – certain features of the act itself other than the value it brings into existence, for example, the fact that it keeps a promise, is just, or is commanded by God or the state. Teleologists believe that there is one and only one basic or ultimate right-making characteristic, namely the comparative value (non-moral) of what is, probably will be, or is intended to be brought into being. Deontologists either deny that this characteristic is right-making at all or they insist that there are other basic or ultimate right-making characteristics as well.

It is clear from the above that in a teleological theory, conduciveness to some goal is the necessary criterion for the rightness of an action, whereas in deontological theory either, this is not the case at all or at least it is not the only and exclusive criterion for judging an action to be right; there are other considerations besides. Now, let us try to categorise the Indian theories of moral obligation and value as teleological and deontological on the basis of the above clarifications regarding the nature of the two theories.

In a way the whole Indian ethical system is deontological, something is *dharma* (duty, obligation or virtue) simply because it is a Vedic law or because the *Dharma Sutras* and *Sastras* prescribe it. This seems to be the temperament of the entire Indian system taken in general. We have seen the definition of morality being advanced more often in terms of what is enjoined by the *Vedas* and *Dharma Sastras*. It is hardly said that what leads to *moksha* is morality, but it is repeatedly said that what is enjoined by the *Vedas*, or what is willed by

God or what marks the imitation of the virtues imbibed by God is morality. The *Mimamsa* clearly says there is no duty other than what is prescribed by the *Vedas*. So something is duty because it is enjoined by the *Vedas* as duty.

The Nyaya-Vaisesika

In the *Vaisesika Sutras*, the very definition of *dharma* is given in terms of ulterior ends like *abhyudaya* (prosperity) and *nihsreyasa* (highest end). It is said that whatever leads to prosperity and the highest end is *dharma*. So here it seems clear that the obligation for *dharma* arises from the twin ends of worldly prosperity and final liberation. Some actions are to be called moral or immoral with reference to whether they lead to the twin ends or not. The *Vaisesika* morality is definitely teleological then. Similarly, the *Nyaya* gives primary importance to *istasadhanata* in determining the obligation of a moral action or a moral law on which some action is based.

The Mimamsa

As opposed to this, the *Mimamsakas* do not take the obligatoriness of moral actions as stemming from the consequence or the end. According to Kumarila, the end or *phala* may be said to determine the motive of the agent, but not the obligation. Obligation is the result of the *vidhi* of which the action in question is an instance. The imperativeness or the obligation of the action is independent of the end or *phala*. The *phala* or consequence is only *pravarttaka*, i.e., a psychological motive, but is not *vidheya*, i.e., the object of a moral imperative. It is a psychological implicate of the moral action, an end as motive being necessary for moral behaviour as for all actions, but it is not a moral implicate of the imperative, which is obligatory independently of the end or consequence. Hence, the end or *phala*, according to Kumarila, forms only a motive to move the agent for action. What makes the action moral or immoral is simply its Vedic sanction or lack of it. The moral obligation of the action follows from the Vedic source without any consideration for the consequence.

The Ramanuja Vedanta

The Visistadvaita system of Ramanuja also comes to be a deontological system on scrutiny insofar as its characterisation as a moral system is concerned. Like other Indian systems, the system of Ramanuja also takes *moksha* to be the ultimate human end. Furthermore, by virtue of believing in *samuccayavada.* Ramanuja gives morality an important place in men's efforts to for attain *moksha*. But, the question is, does conduciveness to *moksha* constitute the necessary condition for an action to be moral? Does the obligation of a moral action follow from the final end of *moksha?* The answer is a clear "no". For the obligation of moral actions in the system of Ramanuja follows from the fact that moral qualities in their absolute and ultimate perfection constitute the essential nature of God and man's duty is simply to imitate or to follow those moral qualities. Thus, man's moral virtues and duties are derivations of God's moral qualities. They are to be observed and followed simply because they represent God's qualities and God wants men to follow the moral qualities that He possesses in a perfect and absolute manner. So, the sanction and authority of morality comes from no less a being than God. Moral qualities imbibed by God in a perfect manner are for us to imitate. In other words, our duty is to behave in a way God would in a similar circumstance. For example, God possesses the moral quality of compassion, so we should be compassionate towards others; God possesses the quality of forgiveness, so we should forgive those who do wrong to us, and so on. In Ramanuja's system, God is regarded as a moral ideal with reference to which man's duties are to be derived or deduced. So man's moral duties follow directly from the moral perfections of God and not from any non-moral end like *moksha.* So, Ramanuja's system also is a deontological system and not a teleological one.

The Samkhya and the Advaita Vedanta

In *Samkhya* and *Advaita Vedanta,* as we have already seen, morality is neither necessary not sufficient for *moksha*. So the question of the obligation of moral actions following from this non-moral end perhaps does not arise. Nevertheless, none of the systems takes moral virtues and duties to be simply valueless. What *Samkhya* criticises in the name of works are mainly the ritualistic acts of the *Vedas*. But, in its turn, *Samkhya* realises the importance of moral virtues following from the *sattvika* nature of man. These moral virtues pave to some extent one's path to *moksha* also. But it is important to realise that these moral virtues do not derive their sanction from their ends, whether *moksha* or anything else. They derive their sanction rather from the metaphysical nature of man.

Man as a psychological being is evolved from *prakrti*. Of the three *gunas* of *prakrti*, *sattva* is the most commendable, because it is the repository of good human qualities. So virtues following from *sattva*, such as kindness, restraint of sense organs, etc., are to be inculcated and followed. Similarly, in *Samakara*, moral virtues do not derive their sanction from *moksha*, although they serve as auxiliaries in the attainment of *moksha*. The essence of *Samkhya Yoga* can be described through Figure 1.1:

Figure 1.1
Essence of Samkhya Yoga

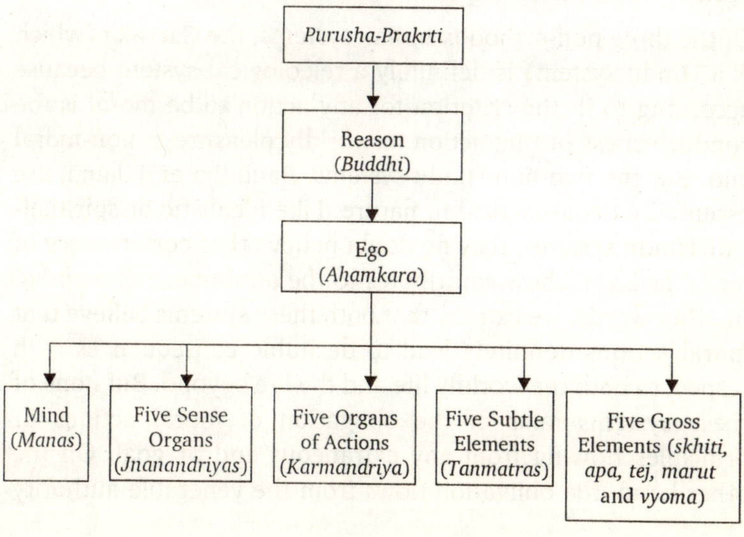

1. *Purusha:* Pure consciousness seemingly comes in contact with *prakrti*
2. *Prakrti:* Indeterminate and imperceptible. It is the equilibrium of the three constituents – *sattwa, raja* and *tama gunas*.

After getting the reflection of the *purusha, prakrti* becomes conscious and agitated. This agitation disturbs the equilibrium of the three constituents of *prakrti* (*sattwa, raja* and *tama*) and thereby evolution becomes operative. First of all, the *sattwa* constituent becomes dominant and reason (*buddhi*) appears. It has cosmic significance and hence is called the great (*mahat*). Although reason is cosmic and above the ego, it is still individual and there are as many reasons as individual egos. The ego (*ahamkara*) evolves out of reason. Depending upon the dominance of one of the three constituents (*gunas*), we get three kinds of ego:

1. *Sattvika ahamkara,*
2. *Rajasika ahamkara,* and
3. *Tamasika ahamkara.*

The Non-orthodox Systems (Carvaka, Buddhism and Jainism)

Of the three non-orthodox Indian systems, the Carvaka (which is a Hindu system) is definitely a teleological system because according to it, the criterion for any action to be moral is the conduciveness of that action to worldly pleasure, a non-moral end. But the two non-Hindu systems, Bauddha and Jaina, are essentially deontological in nature. Like idealistic or spiritualistic Hindu systems, they no doubt believe that performance of moral acts somehow contributes to the attainment of *moksha*. In other words, we can say that both these systems believe that moral actions definitely lead to desirable consequences with respect to both the worldly life and the life beyond. But none of these systems talks of the obligation of moral actions or principles flowing from any extraneous end or goal. On the other hand, the obligation flows from the venerable authority that is bestowed upon the original propounders of the two systems – Lord Buddha and Lord Mahavira.

Thus, despite *moksha* being the ultimate human end towards which all philosophical, religious and moral efforts are supposed to be directed in the Indian tradition, the Indian moral system, by and large, proves to be deontological in nature. And, it is quite natural for it to be so. We have seen that the *Sastras* have been regarded as the primary source and sanction of *dharma* in India. That implies that although the observance of the Sastric *dharma* its naturally and undoubtedly leads to good consequences, moral worth is not to be evaluated in terms of the consequences. Its moral worth is to be determined and assessed only with reference to whether they are

Figure 1.2

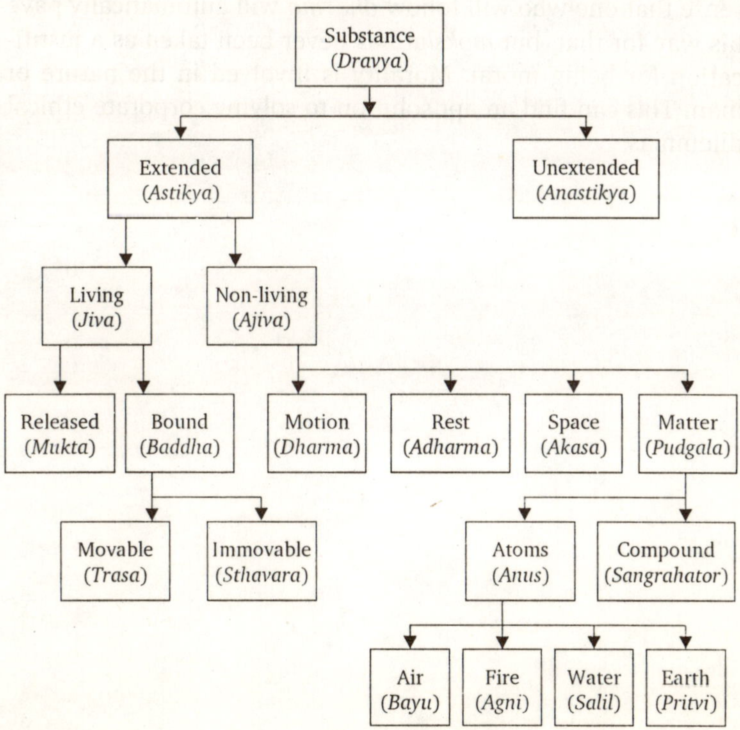

enjoined by the *Sastras*. In other words, *dharma* is *dharma* not because it leads to *moksha*, but because it has been enjoined by authority to be *dharma*. Hence, clearly the overall tone of Indian morality is deontological, implying thereby that *dharma* is to be followed for the reason that it is *dharma* as enjoined by authority.

The philosophy of Jaina is atheistic, realistic and pluralistic. It is an ethics of self-conquest, which does not need God's help or intervention. The Jaina classification may be seen in Figure 1.2.

In the Indian context, man's own nature furnishes a justification for his being moral. Perhaps, this is why most Indian systems prove to be deontological in nature. According to them, *dharma* is to be followed because it is its own justification. *Moksha* has been brought forth as a motivation in the sense that one who will follow *dharma* will automatically pave his way for that, but *moksha* has never been taken as a justification for being moral. Morality is involved in the nature of man. This can find an apt solution to solving corporate ethical dilemmas.

2

Teleology, Deontology and Praxis: The Managerial Perspective

Deontological theories maintain that the concept of duty is in some respects independent of the concept of good and that some actions are right or wrong for reasons other than their consequences. Kantian ethics fall into this category. Kant argues that what makes an action right or wrong is not the sum of its consequences, but the fact that it conforms to moral law.[1] Moral laws of duty demand that people act not only in accordance with duty, but also for the sake of duty. It is not good enough to perform a morally correct action because this could stem from self-interested motives that have nothing to do with morality. Our "masking" in public life also goes hand-in-hand with the statement mentioned above.

Rather, an action is moral if it conforms with moral laws that are based not in institution, conscience or utility, but in pure reason. We can determine moral law by analysing the nature of reason itself and what it means to be a rational being.

Reason has three major characteristics:

1. *Consistency:* Moral actions must not contradict one another.

2. *Universality:* Because reason is the same for all, what is rational to me, is rational to everyone else.
3. *A priori deviation*: It is not based on experience, hence the morality of an action does not depend on its consequences.

A person acts morally if the sole motive for an action is the recognition of moral duty on a valid rule.

In sharp contrast to a deontological position is teleological concept (or utilitarianism). This concept claims that the morality of actions is to be judged by their consequences.

An action is moral if, when compared with any alternative action, it produces the greatest amount of good (or the least possible balance of bad consequences) for the greatest number of people directly or indirectly affected by that action. The maximisation of the good calls for efficiency. It also allows that people might be treated as a means to an end, if the end is the maximisation of the good (or minimisation of the bad) for the greatest number.

The praxis model in the corporate context denotes a set of administrators who seek support from the society they live in and the populace around them. They do not worry about the end and the means as much as they believe that their judgement should be upheld by society. They look for peer support, peer approval and seek shelter in conformity.

Rawls argued that we should look for a conception of justice that nullifies the accidents of natural endowments and contingencies of social circumstances as counters in the quest for political and economic advantages.[2]

His approach, in a sense, is Kantian in that he attempts to desire principles of distributive justice that should be acceptable to all rational people and, hence, universal.

In order to find such principles, Rawls suggested we perform a thought experiment. Suppose all people are behind a "veil of ignorance", where we know we are rational beings and that we value our own good, but we do not know if we are male or female, rich or poor, talented or untalented, white or black and so on. What principles would we call just or fair if we did not know what place we would have in society (or organisation in the corporate context)? In such circumstances, Rawls argues people would agree on two principles of justice:

1. Each person is to have an equal right to the most extensive basic liberty compatible with similar liberty for others.
2. Social and economic inequalities are to be arranged so that they are both (a) reasonably expected to be to everyone's advantage, and (b) attached to positions and offices open to all.

Now, obviously, there are some difficulties with all these theories. It is often said that covertly appeal to utilisation (teleological) consequences in order to demonstrate the rightness of actions, particularly when there is a clash of moral rules. Utilitarianism has to cope with the problem of lack of knowledge of all consequences, of weighing together different kinds of good and evil and of the issue of unjust consequences. Rawls' second principle can be attacked as being too strong (as long as equal opportunities exist, why should rewards have to take the place of producing benefits for the least advantaged groups in society?) or too weak (in that it would allow the very rich to get very much richer as long as the very poor got a little less poor). But leaving these on one side, we want to take the central tenets of each theory and evaluate behavioural deviations.

Deontology: Treat people with respect and as ends in their own right, not solely as means to others' ends. Any moral rule must be capable of being consistently universalised, respect the dignity of persons and be acceptable to rational beings. Any action performed out of self-interest is not moral.

Teleology: The greatest good to the greatest number allows people to be treated as means to ends if it is to the advantage of the majority. Actions should be judged in terms of their consequences (Legge, 1998).

Praxis: This school suggests a kind of need for acceptance. The word praxis has been borrowed from Marxist literature to denote the process of conversion of theory to practice. It signifies a conversion of their (the manager's) value system into managerial decision-making (Sadri and Jayashree, 1999).[3]

Rawlsian: The good must be distributed with mutual consultation and so that no organisational stakeholders* are complete losers, while others are clear winners. Management must place priority on the long-term interests of stockholders and the survival of the organisation.

We may recall here the theory of Pareto optimality in the social context. Pareto optimality means that there is no way to rearrange endowments, production and consumption so that all economic agents are simultaneously better off. This theory sounds very nice (Ray, 1998) and at some level it is, but it is perfectly compatible with the idea that some people are getting very little of the economic prosperity.[4] The best way to understand this is to think of dividing a cake between two people. As long as one is not throwing any of the cake away, any division is Pareto optimal, including the one in which one person eats all of it.

On its own, as Sen observes, the Pareto criterion can be seen as capturing a particular aspect of welfarism, to wit, a unanimous ranking of individual utilities must be adequate for overall social ranking of the respective states.[5] In fact, Sen further clarifies, the policy use of the Pareto criterion to go beyond welfarism and embrace

---

* The popular version of the stakeholder theory (e.g., Evan and Freeman, 1988) asserts that organisations have stakeholders, that is groups and individuals that potentially benefit from (or are harmed by) an organisation's actions. Stakeholders of an organisation might comprise, for example, not just shareholders, but management, other employees, customers, suppliers and the local community. The stakes of each group are reciprocal since each can affect the others in terms of harms and benefits as well as rights and duties. This principle of reciprocity leads to two further principles:

(i) The organisation should be managed for the benefit of its stakeholders and the groups must participate in decisions that affect their welfare.

(ii) Management must act as a "do-gooder" agent for the survival of the firm.

consequentialism (teleological philosophy) is implicitly but firmly demanded.[6]

Sen's "self-goal choice" can be best understood in terms of the Prisoners' Dilemma.[7] Two prisoners have committed a crime, for which the police is interrogating them. Each prisoner has two options: He can cooperate with his fellow prisoner and refuse to divulge any evidence or he can defect and reveal all. Thus, the strategy set of each prisoner consists of two strategies: cooperate or defect. Two persons with different moral-goal-ordering can be involved in a Prisoners' Dilemma game, and if they both pursue self-goal choice, then, commented Sen,[8] all the usual results will follow. The issue of the correspondence between goals and choice arises not merely in the general context of consequentialism, but also in that of assessing the action implications of one's own goals in the light of the goals of others.

Figure 2.1

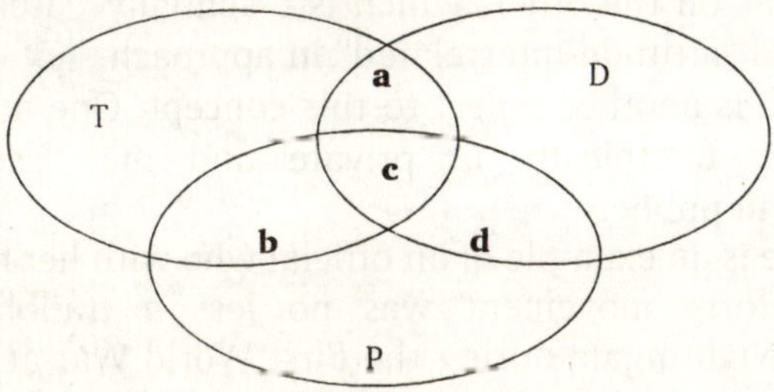

Ethical "overlaps" or "grey areas" of ethics are those aspects of behaviour which cannot be accommodated in any of three categories: teleological, deontological and the praxis. Now considering the occurrence of "overlaps", we find the following four situations, which are very important when studying ethics (Figure 2.1):

1. *Situation a:* When the teleological concept of ethics mixes up with deontological views.
   (ends + means are important),

2. *Situation b*: When praxis theory gets intermingled with the teleological stream.
   (conformity + ends are important),
3. *Situation c:* Where there is a grand combination of all three "schools".
   (ends + means + praxis combine and unite).
4. *Situation d:* When praxis theory mixes up with the deontological concept.
   (conformity + means are important).

Observing all four situations mentioned, it is obvious that Situation **c** is the best; next is Situation **d** and then comes Situation **a** and Situation **b** in preferential order.

Solving ethical dilemmas by choosing "in-between" choices (that conform to the Venn diagram of the set theory in mathematics), a person need not resort to any of the four "overlapping" segments at a time. At one point, he may behave according to situation **b**, at another, situation **c**. Why he does so? To solve the ethical dilemma on the one hand and to justify his "image" on the other, which is essentially "situational" in nature and "attitude-interrelated" in approach.

There is another aspect to this concept. One may behave completely unethically in private and may use "ethical masking" in public.

There is an example of an official who with her far-sighted prison reform movement was no less a trailblazer than Florence Nightingale during the First World War at one point of time, but at another point, she turned out to be unethical when she sought her daughter's admission in Delhi through a medical quota, which virtually thwarted the chances of the promising children of other government officials working in a particular state government of obtaining medical quotas.

Are these two opposite behavioural expositions – one working at a "personal" level and the other at a societal level – the same or different? Affection for a daughter may lead a parent to go to any extent, but at the same time, at a macro level, the Upanishadic dictum of *damyata, datta, dayadhavam* (self-control, charity and compassion) may nurture the mind of the same person to help the oppressed.

Thus, situational behaviour can break ethical barriers at one level and resort to some at another.

This reminds the author of an otherwise ethical government official who succumbed to the pressure of paying forty thousand rupees as a donation to get his son admitted in one of the best schools in Kolkata.

This is true of Indian managers as well. "Ethical masking" (or "unmasking" for that matter) is, thus, necessarily designed for two factors:

1. Situation (to "manage", "combat" or "overcome" the situation), and
2. Attitude-interrelatedness (a person may hesitate to drop a coin into the hands of a beggar on the street, but seldom minds drawing cheques for an international charity home to earn "image").

Thus, the question that baffles us is whether it is interrelatedness or inter-separatedness? It is interrelatedness *per se*, because there lies a fundamental relationship between these two extremes. To examine this problem, let us assume a situation where a person behaves rudely with his wife at home, but changes his behaviour completely when accompanying her to a party.

The "wall" that differentiates the two different kinds of attitude of the same person at different points of time with the same person denotes a conscious attitudinal infringement area (CAIA), where moral dilemmas take birth to bridge the two different kinds of attitude to give way to attitude-interrelatedness.

Most ethical decisions inviting ethical "overlaps" as mentioned come from this area.

Let us put forward an example in the corporate context.

A manager may behave in a different manner with his juniors and workers, but may change his approach "consciously" while "dialoguing" with a superior.

This example serves to summarise two important types of behaviour:

1. Controlled conscious behaviour.
2. Uncontrolled conscious behaviour.

A graph will illustrate the proposition (Figure 2.2):

Figure 2.2

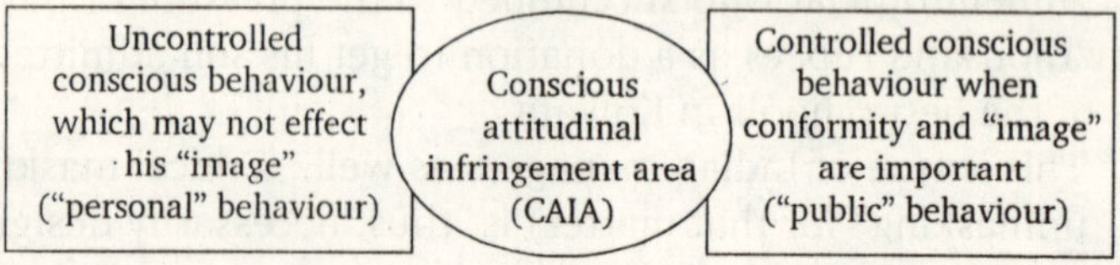

The conscious attitudinal infringement area contrives the two into two extremes, yet takes the both into its field, thereby giving a feature of interrelatedness and not as one may observe, apparently.

Before going deep into the topic of "how to make both ends meet" (meaning to be ethical both in public and private life), let us take a look at what Immanuel Kant says:

> "Enlightenment is man's emergence from his self-incurred immaturity. The motto of enlightenment is therefore: Sapereaude (think for yourself). Have courage to use your own understanding?"[9]

G.W.F. Hegel puts forward the following:

> "From the inner revolution, there emerges the actual revolution of the actual word, the new shape of consciousness, absolute freedom".[10]

The most defensible approach to addressing the problem of establishing normative standards is offered by critical theory (Reed, 1998).[11] Critical theory adopts a procedural approach to normative theory that is based upon the notion of discourse (Reed, 1998b).[12] The foundation of this approach is the theory of communicative action.[13] The basic premise of this theory is that reason admits of two distinct forms:

1. Instrumental reason (pursuing goals and interests), and

2. Communicative reason (attempting to reach mutual understanding).

A distinguishing characteristic of moral discourse vis-à-vis ethical discourse is that it allows for universal validity claims. The reason for this difference lies in the fact that morality involves a purely procedural process while ethical reasoning relates to our conception of the good life (Reed, 1998b).[14]

In this context, as we perceive, there is a functional relationship between morality and ethical reasoning and the two cannot be mutually exclusive "events".

In order to "reinforce" to narrow the gap between the two ends – personal behaviour and public behaviour (i.e., ethical masking) – there should be a harmonisation paradigm. This means leading a moral life in person and behaving ethically in public. This is how one can liberate oneself from Kantian "self-incurred immaturity".

Corporate Scenario in India in General: Whither Values?

Business Today (BT), in its July 22 to August 6, 1995 issue, conducted a survey on chief executive officers (CEOs) of both Indian and transnational companies under the title "Ethical Enigma" and collected responses from them on ethics in the corporate sector, its influence, erosion and consequences. The survey pinpointed these issues by asking some pertinent questions: How ethical is corporate India? How unwaveringly are CEOs committed to running principled organisations? How deeply in their estimation has the moral rot set in? As business is increasingly stained by practices ranging from the blatantly illegal – ramping share prices, tax evasion, embezzlement and diversion of corporate funds, bribery and kickbacks, underhand foreign exchange deals etc. – to the palpably deceitful – what are the most unethical practices in use today?

To obtain the response, *BT* structured the following questions:

1. What is the current level of business ethics?
2. Have ethical standards declined of late?

3. How is liberalisation affecting ethics?
4. What are the factors responsible for poor corporate ethics?
5. Why cannot unethical business practices be checked?
6. Are unethical practices essential to succeed in corporate India?
7. Is India's environment to blame for poor ethics?
8. What and how unethical are today's unethical practices?
9. What really distinguishes unethical acts from illegal ones?
10. How do Indian business ethics compare with global ethics?
11. Are Indian ethics fundamentally different from western ethics?

For conducting the survey, *BT* chose a representation of fourteen companies from different important regions of the country: Delhi (27), Mumbai (15), Kolkata (22), Chennai (21) and Bangalore (15). There was a mix of transnational and Indian companies as forty-three transnational and fifty-seven Indian firms responded. The survey was conducted by administering a structured questionnaire to eliminate the need for face-to-face interaction with the respondent, allowing CEOs to respond in private to the sensitive issues raised.

In response to the first question, 66 per cent of the CEOs found their (and their peers') ethical standards hovering between average and very low. Another 17 per cent considered corporate India's morals barely above passing grade. And, 69 per cent of Indian CEOs condemned today's principles as against 63 per cent of transnational CEOs.

It is interesting to note that Indian have not made up their mind regarding the second question. But the contradictions between the two viewpoints are acute:

1. 46 per cent of Indian CEOs deplored the declining standards.
2. But 40 per cent of transnational CEOs celebrated an improvement.

(The question remains: How is this possible when 63 per cent of transnational, meaning the majority, condemned the current level of business ethics? Either they were overzealous or the Indian CEOs were cynical.)

The question of liberalisation and its effect on ethics draws a picture that is not unanimous. While 6 per cent believed reforms would make corporate India more unethical. Not surprisingly, 81 per cent of transnational favoured the cause, but a high 22 per cent were caught between pre-and post-reforms, as there is little to choose when it comes to the question of maintaining ethical standards in the face of liberalisation.

The next question in the survey consisted of eleven factors that contribute towards poor corporate ethics and asked the respondents to prioritise these factors. Their choices were:

1. Work culture,
2. Licence raj,
3. Systematic corruption,
4. High taxes,
5. Protected economy,
6. Archaic business laws,
7. Government over-employment,
8. Lack of competition,
9. Absence of consumerism,
10. Poor law implementation, and
11. Low purchasing power.

All the CEOs blamed the systematic corruption the most (82 per cent), followed by the licence raj (66 per cent), poor law implementation (59 per cent), high taxes (58 per cent) and archaic business laws (44 per cent).

Both Indian and transnational came to a consensus on the three major factors responsible for poor corporate ethics:

1. Systematic corruption (Indian 79 per cent; transnational CEOs 86 per cent),
2. Poor law implementation (Indian 53 per cent; transnational CEOs 87 per cent), and
3. Licence raj (Indian 56 per cent and transnational CEOs 79 per cent).

Concentrating on the question why unethical business practices cannot be checked, few considered that the law was weak. One third believed that it promotes, instead of preventing, corrupt practices. However, most agreed that feeble implementation is to be blamed. 37 per cent of transnational and 22 per cent of Indian CEOs blamed the law for encouraging unethical business practices.

About the question of ethics being practised in corporate India, a majority 36 per cent of all believed that ethical practices are essential for success in the Indian corporate world, 26 per cent thought that such practices had some relevance, 25 per cent believed they would lead fairly and curiously, 13 per cent of all the CEOs were of the view that unethical practices were absolutely essential to succeed in corporate India. Dividing them, 15 per cent of Indian CEOs and 9 per cent of transnational CEOs believed that unethical practices were absolutely necessary to succeed, while 34 per cent of Indian CEOs and 40 per cent of transnational CEOs were totally against unethical practices. 29 per cent of Indian CEOs and 23 per cent of transnational CEOs hovered around "somewhat" and the remaining 22 per cent of Indian CEOs and 28 per cent of transnational CEOs fell within the category of "fairly".

Regarding the unethical nature of today's practices, cheating the government and employees by way of not paying taxes and not depositing provident fund payments, respectively, top the unethical practices scale. However, transnational disagreed with their Indian counterparts on some factors. They censured ramping of share prices almost as much as they did evasion of taxes or non-deposition of provident fund dues.

On what really distinguishes unethical acts from illegal ones, Indian were not deluding themselves by equating unethical actions with transgressing the law. All of them agreed that it was possible to stay legally clean and still break the code of corporate conduct. While more than half believed that being unethical was all about flouting morals, only 5 per cent transnational CEOs felt that unethical practices shatter the spirit and not the letter of the law.

Putting Indian business ethics with global standards on a comparative scale, we find that only 4 per cent of Indian CEOs and 3 per cent of transnational CEOs were of the view that this issue merits comparisons, while a majority of both the groups (47 per cent and 71 per cent, respectively) thought Indian business ethical standards were lower than those prevalent globally.

Lastly, 62 per cent of all CEOs agreed that the difference in ethical benchmarks between India and the West are generated by a divergence of fundamentals. But 38 per cent opposed the notion – it is far from being universally accepted.

Analysis

Taking a summary of all the observations made by the CEOs, a composite analysis the can be drawn thus:

1. The ethical standards in corporate India lie between average and very low. The standards can barely scale the passing grade.
2. Owing to a weak legal system, unethical practices cannot be checked.
3. Cheating of both the government and employees tops the list of unethical practices in the Indian corporate world.
4. Systematic corruption is to be blamed the most, followed by the licence raj, poor law implementation, high taxes and archaic business laws.
5. It is observed that the ethical standards in corporate India are lower than global standards.

   Some pertinent questions:

   (a) Does not the manifestation of unethical practices in the Indian corporate world mirror the "lower self" in a person?
   (b) Is this culture specific? Or global?
   (c) How can one solve the "dichotomised" dilemma of "personal behaviour" and "public behaviour"?
   (d) What are the ways to "reinforce" CAIA to narrow this gap?
   (e) How can one achieve "critical behavioural positivity"?

In order to answer these questions, let us first start from the point where we began, i.e., looking into the three basic concepts of ethical philosophy, namely, deontological, teleological (utilitarianism) and the praxis.

This situation calls for our theory of CAIA to look into the behavioural aspects of corporate managers in the Indian context.

India, like Japan, is culture-specific. But Japan is held as a country that has fostered "systematic departures from self-interested behaviour in the direction of duty, loyalty and goodwill" (Sen, 1987).[15] India, on the other hand, has tarnished her image over a period of more than fifty years through systematic corruption, butchered public sector units, sluggish bureaucracy and rampant misappropriation at almost all levels, and the beleaguered corporate sector cannot be excluded from this list.

Taking the question on behavioural aspects with respect to corporate activity, one may go deep into an integrated area, which is often dichotomised into binary expression – subjective and objective. If a system fails, if work culture in general sails at its lowest ebb, if corrupt practices outshine moral nuances, if an all-pervading quest for money takes over the ethical foundations of today's corporate world in India in particular, it is nothing but the manifestation of the "moral failure" on part of the "collective unconscious". According to the theory of Carl Jung, it is the "collective unconscious" that is the origin of "individual" consciousness. Human intelligence has two components:

1. The reflection of the subconscious on one hand and
2. The experience of the external world on the other.

The Buddhist view has expressed the dichotomy between the subjective and the objective in a more analytical way. According to it:

1. Man becomes attached to his scanty memories because he in practice confuses these with his own self, as if there were not to be found outside him, before and after him impressions, destinies, memories fairer or richer than his

own and to which he will never have access; and as if a mental image, whatever its value, could forever be identified with one's immortal personality.

2. Man is incapable of viewing an object from all sides at once or under all its aspects – it is impossible for him to enjoy at the same time every aspect of a precious thing or of a beloved being; in carnal ecstasy (a baser instinct for all earthly desires and a prime driver for resorting to amoral or unethical doings), a creature can no longer enjoy any visual perception of form, and this is an impoverishment even while foreshadowing their extinction of the soul in God.

The foregoing considerations bring us closer to the Vedantic idea or even Sufism, i.e., the idea of the unreality of the world.

> The Vedanta preaches the ideal; and the ideal, as we know, is always far ahead of the real, of the practical, as we may call it. There are two tendencies in human nature: one to harmonise the ideal with the life, and the other to elevate the life to the ideal.
>
> Now if any man comes to preach to me a certain ideal, the first step towards which is to give up selfishness, to give up self-enjoyment, I think that is impractical. But when a man brings an ideal which can be reconciled with my selfishness, I am glad and jump at it. – You see how we all use this practical world for things we like and can do. Therefore I will ask you to understand that Vedanta, though it is intensely practical, is always so in the sense of the ideal. In one word, this ideal is that you are divine, "Thou art That" (emphasis added). These lines are from the *Complete Works of Swami Vivekananda*, Vol. 2, p. 294, Kolkata.

Sufism comprises the same doctrine. It emphasises that the world is an imaginary form, a diffused shadow of the Infinite... The imagination produces objective phenomena having no real existence; in the same way, this world has no substantial reality, but is only a play of shadows or a game. All is penetrated by the Absolute Being in its infinite perfection. There are many numbers, but only one alone counts....The house has been left empty, except for the truth, because the world disappeared in an instant.

Considering all these ideas propagated by Buddhism, Vedanta and Sufism, one believes that the spirituo-technical approach makes a fundamental shift from the current reductionist (lean manufacturing, outsourcing and other concepts emphasising lower costs, faster production, etc.), fragmentist, materialist paradigm to one which recognises relationships, consciousness and spirit as the right approach.

Someswarananda prepared a model of decision styles based on Vedantic ideas of human behaviour or inclination (Figure 2.3).[16] According to his model, managers display the following orientation of *karma* (work), *jnana* (knowledge), *yoga* (consciousness) or *bhakti* (devotion).

1. The work-oriented (*karma*) manager is a no-nonsense person, is organised and a "workaholic".
2. The knowledge-oriented (*jnana*) manager is basically an analyser. He always asks for logic, facts and figures.

Figure 2.3

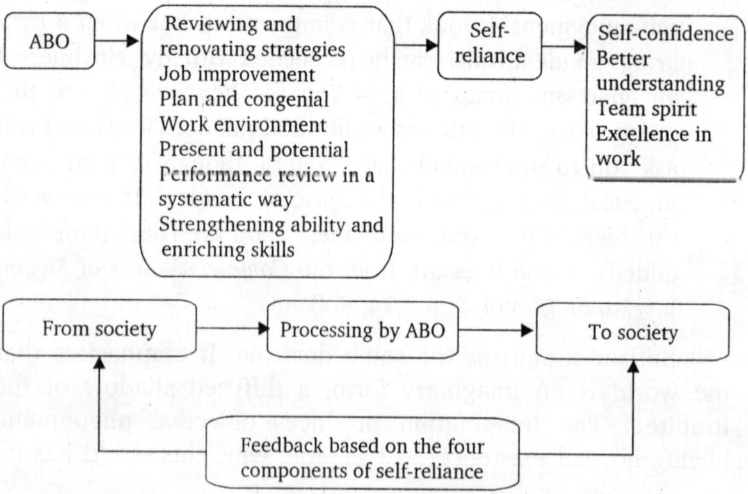

3. The consciousness-oriented (*yoga*) manager is very creative. He is always charged with new ideas, new innovations, new approaches and is always on the move.
4. The devotion-oriented (*bhakti*) manager gives importance to the feelings of employees. He is kind to his juniors and empathy driven towards his peers.

In order to "reinforce" CAIA to narrow the gap between personal behaviour and public behaviour and leading a moral life to behave ethically in public, there is a harmonisation approach which denotes that there is a direct correspondence between man's inner life of thoughts, feelings and emotions (i.e., CAIA), and the circumstances and events in his outer environment. The "reinforcement" process of CAIA can be "engineered" and "implemented" through three stages:

1. Aspiration,
2. Consecration, and
3. Self-introspection.

Aspiration forms the basic attitude because a manager has to take the decision with intense aspiration, deepest devotion, perfect objectivity and strong conviction towards welfarism. These values should manifest in his personal life as well towards his spouse, children, parents, relatives and friends.

Consecration means complete surrender in communion. Let the manager consecrate to the Divinity his institution, organisational hierarchy, all systems and sub-systems, manpower, himself and, finally, his family. By consecration, one leaves oneself wholly to the care and charge of the Divine. Then faith develops, conviction comes in and communion grows.

Through self-introspection, "reinforcement" of CAIA can be "engineered" to bridge the gap between the two ends by way of following a fundamental maxim: "Search thine own self first", for any fault, faux pas, misdemeanour, public or personal, for any conflict – we have to look within, go deep into our inner being and discover if we are on the wrong side or on the right. This is a sojourn within us, a kind of invisible journey.

These exercises do not reside in a castle of clouds. These practices or these "mental modules" have some concrete foundational base. In this context, Japan's corporate giant, Matsushita's management philosophy may be taken into consideration as a glaring example. The management philosophy of this corporate giant hinges on seven basic principles:

1. National service through industry,
2. Fairness,
3. Harmony and cooperation,
4. Struggle for betterment,
5. Courtesy and humility,
6. Adjustment and assimilation, and
7. Gratitude.

Matsushita believes that the inherent preferences of organisations are clarity, certainty and perfection. The inherent nature of human relationships involves ambiguity, uncertainty and imperfections. How one honours, balances and integrates the needs of both is the way through "reinforcement engineering".

Darryl Reed has tried recently to investigate the extent to which corporations in India, have conformed to the defensive normative standards in their various dealings and to identify the factors which have influenced their rate of non-conformity.[17] Reed has addressed two key issues concerning the ethical obligations of corporations in promoting development. The first of these questions, the nature of such ethical obligations, has been examined by drawing upon German critical theory, which we mentioned earlier. The second, more practical, question involved the conditions under which firms were likely to assume obligations to development and make an effective contribution.

The outcome of the research concludes that from the perspective of pragmatic reasoning, the benefits that accrue to the companies are important. To maximise the benefits, they may require only the perception of community and social development activity and not necessarily the results. By contrast, ethical motivation provides a much firmer basis for companies to be primarily concerned with the results of their activities. For this reason, ethical motivation provides a much firmer basis for companies to assume their responsibilities to development. In doing so, Reed summed up, they (companies) provide an important example and challenge to other companies and demonstrate the key role of human values in the corporate sector living up to the responsibilities to development.[18] Daniel Sherrick reported that one company was severely hurt by its refusal to keep its employees informed on the progress of negotiations to sell off an operating unit.[19] Rumours about potential lay-offs and firings hurt the morale and resulted in strained relations between management and the workers.

This example, taken from a US-based company, makes it clear that many managerial decisions bear ethical components that relate to the unique needs of the employees. Failures to consider the impact of these decisions relating to employees could have long-term implications more severe than anticipated.

There are some additional dimensions to ethical dilemmas in the corporate context. Often, one may be in a position of being able to accomplish a goal for the "greater good" of the organisation or society, if short-run ethical considerations are ignored. In such a case, the end is important, but at the cost of means.

Managers are often faced with a similar ethical problem of trying to determine the "right thing" to do in making a decision. In the western context, the trend toward downsizing may make it necessary to lay off a sizeable number of a company's most skilled and dedicated workers to save costs, but is it necessary to be done at all? There lies the normative question that haunts the manager.

Ethical dimensions may also affect the very manner in which a company does business. For example, it may be easier to lower quality control standards to save costs than it is to completely redesign a product to meet the threat of emerging market competition, but do customers have the right to know that what they are buying today may not be as safe as what they bought yesterday? Is it ethical not to tell customers that quality standards have been lowered?

Ethics do not apply only to managers. Employees at all levels must deal with ethical issues.

Thus, numerous ethical considerations relate to human resource decision-making. Many decisions involve ethical components that may be more serious, than the immediate situation at hand due to their impact on the organisation's personnel. Other decisions are difficult because their ethical implications are not always clear. It is often hard to know the ethical norms outside of one's own culture, or to understand the relationship between ethics and the law. The corporate executives play a central role in the ethical considerations and the employees often place them in the position of being the ethical watchdogs. This role not only includes instituting policies and monitoring compliance, but also serving as investigator and judge. Therefore, there should not be any "moral failure" on the part of corporate executives in playing this role effectively.

Again, we may discover that it is the manifestation of the "lower self" in person which has resulted in unethical practices in the Indian corporate context. Chakraborty, in a study of 2,000 Indian managers at the director level, divided their traits into four types:[20]

1. Values weak, skills weak.
2. Values strong, skills strong.
3. Skills weak, values strong.
4. Values weak, skills strong.

He found that most Indian managers (more than 70 per cent of the sample) believed that the majority fell into the values weak, skills strong category.

Further, these manifested traits are definitely culture-specific. Against the backdrop of Asian countries like Japan and Korea, where "nationalist fervour" against American companies put them on a competitive scale or sometimes even on the cutting edge, Indian companies can hardly find their names in the international market, except in industries such as tea and raw materials like iron ore and manganese and precious stones and gems, even after fifty years of independence, publicity for which event soared to such a height that even auto-rickshaws sported stickers that boasted of it. The spent-force of the colonial "babus" took resort in excuses of having built castles in the sand, producing paper tigers, middlemen and swindlers at the cost of development.

What are the specific crises which are whipping off the moral dimensions of life, bogging true human spirit into the quagmire of corrupt practice in a country that once produced Tagore, Vivekananda and Gandhi?

The Indian corporate sector is today facing a five-point crisis:

1. Crisis of leadership,
2. Crisis of mobility,
3. Crisis of focussing,
4. Crisis of empowerment, and
5. Crisis of vision.

Therefore, in order to come out of there crises, the main emphasis should be laid on:

Defining the Role of the Organisation

1. Setting goals both particular and general (particularity means the objectives of various departments/units which will ultimately culminate in the general goal; general goal means the main aim for achievement by the organisation)
2. Pointing out the focus, i.e., the gap between the mission and the general goal, and
3. Finding out various solutions to bridge the gap.

In order to augment the criteria mentioned above, we developed a model called action by objective (ABO). This theory (Das Gupta, 1995) exemplifies a method of self-control and the way of fixing targets with reference to one's own strengths and weaknesses to execute the programme.[21] It comprises the sequential conduct of the following functions:

1. Reviewing and renovating strategies,
2. Providing a job-improvement plan,
3. Using present and potential performance reviews in a systematic way, and
4. Strengthening the ability and enriching the skills of the human resource through effective training and development.

In the ABO approach, the objectives are handed down with no spirit of authoritarianism, but the process should essentially be participatory. As a tool for self-appraisal and self-development, it moves towards self-reliance (in Indian philosophy, it means *moksha* – the way to becoming independent step-by-step), which has four components:

1. Self-confidence,
2. Better understanding,
3. Team spirit, and
4. Excellence of work.

This again, in turn, as per the systems approach, serves as "feedback elements" in a process of "taking from society" and "giving to society". The holistic approach increases the credibility of the review results and performance levels in the participatory system under which "processing" is guided by ABO objectives.

The ABO approach focusses on the treatment programme which involves all the people of the organisation in how the goal can be achieved or the gap can be bridged through self-management teams (SMTs) in various units as against the western HR strategy model, which ultimately stresses on individual achievement rather than group achievement – a crucial factor that has been underlined in the SMT model. The SMT model encompasses autonomy and creative joy that motivates people more than anything else to produce better results.

Further, ABO plans focus on team-building, for which shared vision building, systematic thinking, building "mental models", empowering people and inspiring commitment, enabling better and positive results are to be established and augmented through a "designed learning process" and the consciousness approach.

Thirdly, periodic reviews of the training programmes in the ABO model consist of:

1. Reaction of participants, i.e., their response towards the programme and beyond that,
2. Learning, i.e., participants' intellectual assimilation of the concepts, ideas and principles of the training programme,
3. Behaviour changes, i.e., whether the training caused people to alter their behaviour on the job,
4. Impact of organisational effectiveness, i.e., whether the modified behaviour caused positive results, and
5. Subjective and objective criteria, i.e., subjective criteria call for the opinion of participants and objective criteria relate to the effects of training by measuring specific outcomes.

Finally, the model results in three immediate goal achievement factors, namely:

1. Direction setting,
2. Resolution of conflicts, and
3. Team spirit.

These three factors culminate in ultimate goal achievement, i.e., the self-reliance of halo from which the following four result-oriented factors can be diffused:

1. Knowledge based performance,
2. Value-based management,
3. Development forward excellence, and
4. Shared goals.

For understanding the "bridge factor" between these two dimensions of strategic model building, namely the immediate goal achievement and the ultimate goal achievement within the corporate sector in India, the harmonisation paradigm, the key element to this approach, hinges mainly on four attributes, namely vision, mission, values and programmes.

Vision

This indicates the legacy it would like to pass on to its succeeding generation of leaders – it is a statement which inspires its employees with a dream, a goal and generates pride in them. Alacrity Foundation, engaged in housing and electronics, formulated its vision as "to try and prove that organised business, when deeply committed to values, is best equipped to lead society to a better life". Vision formulation of power management can be visualised through Figure 2.4.

Figure 2.4

Vision Formulation

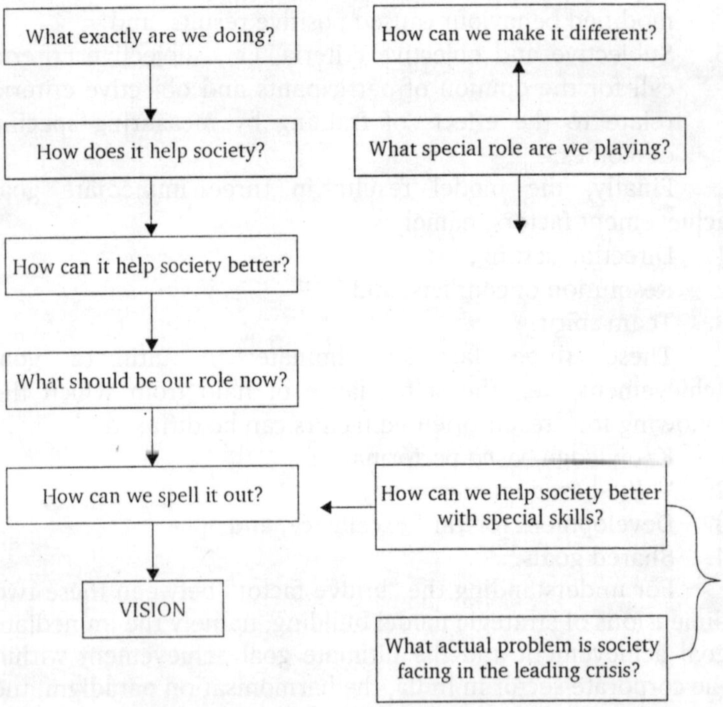

Mission

While a vision denotes a broad, general picture, a mission hones it to focus and concentrates on a particular area. Two organisations may have the same vision, but should have different missions. Figure 2.5 suggests how to formulate a mission:

Figure 2.5
Formulating a Mission

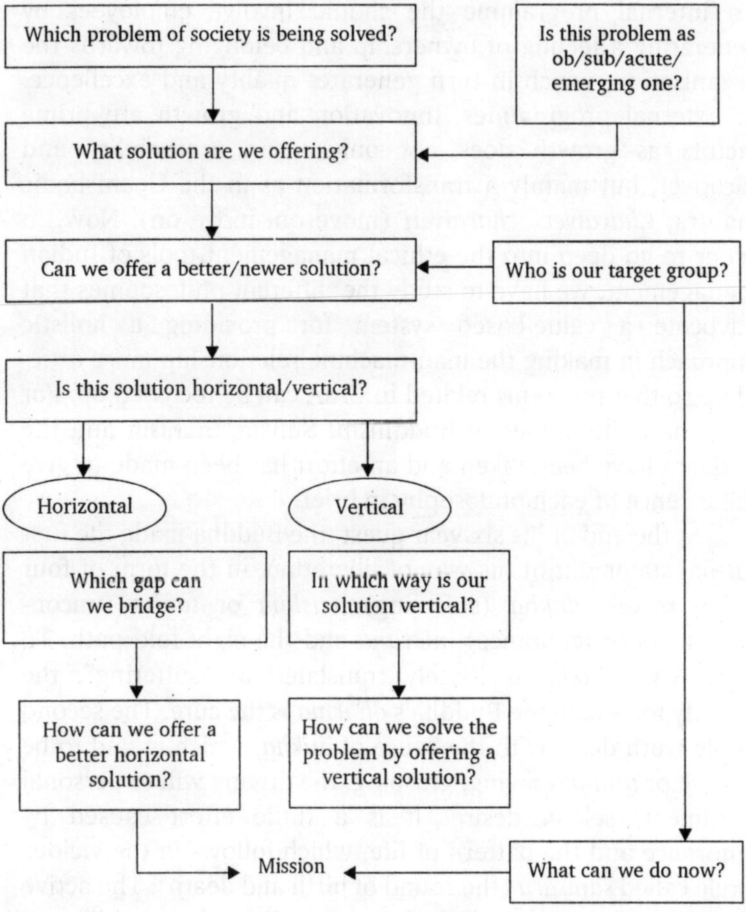

Values

Values indicate the relationship one has with others. The suggestion in the Upanishads, *Saha nau bhunaktu* (Let us all share together), implies cooperation, combined benefits for oneself, collaborates and society, trust and a desire for others' success.

Programmes

There are two aspects to programmes: internal and external. An internal programme the should involve employees by generating a feeling of ownership and belonging towards the organisation, which in turn generates quality and excellence. In external programmes, innovation and growth are prime factors as growth does not only mean profitability and turnover, but mainly a transformation as in the Upanishadic mantra, *Charaiveti, charaiveti* (move on, move on). Now, in order to go deep into the ethical management tools of Indian management, we have to study the different philosophies that advocate a value-based system for providing a holistic approach in making the man-machine relationship more articulate so that problems related to CAIA can be focussed on. For this, the philosophies of Buddhism, Sufism, Sikhism and the Vedanta have been taken and an effort has been made to give the essence of each philosophy in brief.

At the end of his six-year quest, the Buddha made the first formal statement of his way of liberation, in the form of four noble truths: *dukha* (suffering), *trishna* or *tanha* (unconsciousness or ignorance), *nirvana* and the eight-fold path. To start with, *dukha* is loosely translated as "suffering", the malady for which the Buddha's *dharma* is the cure. The second noble truth deals with the cause of *dukha*, which is said to be *trishna* or *tanha:* craving, grasping, the driving will to personal fulfilment, selfish desire. It is a futile effort caused by ignorance and the pattern of life, which follows in the vicious circle called *samsara* (the round of birth and death). The active principle of the "round" is known as *karma* or conditional action, action that is arising from a motive and seeking a result – the type of action which always requires the necessity for further action.

Nirvana, the third nobel truth, answers the question: Can suffering be avoided? Buddhism firmly believes that suffering can be avoided when the nature of ego is perceived. This state is called nirvana, which arises spontaneously when the impossibility of ego-fulfilment has been perceived. The fourth nobel truth describes the eight-fold path, i.e., the values of the Buddha's *dharma*, the method by which unconsciousness is brought to an end. The transformation from *dukha* to *nirvana*. The eight-fold path consists of:

1. *Samyag-drishti* – complete view,
2. *Samyag-samkalpa* – complete aspiration,
3. *Samyag-vak* – complete truthful speech,
4. *Samyag-karmanta* – complete action,
5. *Samyag-jiva* – complete vocation,
6. *Samyag-vyayama* – complete application,
7. *Samyag-smriti* – complete recollectedness, and
8. *Samyag-samadhi* – complete contemplation.

On the other hand, Sufism has gained an oriental flavour from having been so long protected by Islam, but the natural Sufi may be as common in the West as in the East and may come dressed as a general, a peasant, a merchant – anything. To be "in the world, but not of it" – free from ambition, greed, intellectual pride, blind obedience to custom or awe of persons higher in rank – that is the Sufi's ideal. Sufis respect the rituals of religion in so far as these further social harmony, but broaden religion's doctrinal basis wherever possible and define its myths in a higher sense. The spiritual stages through which the Sufis pass are:

1. *Talab* (yearning): For union with God.
2. *Ishq* (love): One has to give up desire for name and fame altogether. Even all faith and virtue must be burnt off on love's altar.
3. *Marfat* (enlightenment): To see the Ultimate Him as the supreme in every particle.

4. *Istaghrak* or *Fana* (absorption): "Come to my help for without Thee I am lost".
5. *Tanhid* (unity consciousness): Experiencing God permeating all as (timeless) unity amidst multiplicity (in time).
6. *Hairat* (amazement): It is a stage when the seeker sees the glorious sight that strikes him dumb and it is a state when one walketh, talketh, feeleth and speaketh as in a dream, yet no mere somnambulism, but stern reality that leaves an impression for life and paves the way to further spiritual advance.
7. *Fuqr wa Fana* (annihilation): Of ego, the lower self and rebirth into the greater self-absorption into the Lord and unity.

In the history of Sufi mysticism, the contribution of Jalaluddin Rumi is epoch-making. Like other mystics, Rumi also believes that reason cannot give us knowledge of the ultimate truth, the noumenal reality, reason can know only phenomena or appearances. Reason can never go beyond the subjective and the objective and as such, it can never realise the fundamental unity of all existence. The pure heart of the perfect man can be compared with a mirror which reflects whatever comes before it.

Sikhism accepted some of the basic doctrines of Hinduism, enlarging and deepening their meaning, and rejected others which were out of harmony with an integrated view of life. It can be seen that the Sikh religion is strictly monotheistic, believing in nothing but the one Supreme God – absolute, yet all pervading, the eternal, the creator. The two basic postulates of Sikhism are that life is not sinful in its origin, but having emanated from a pure source, remains pure in its essence even in life. Secondly, the world is not suffering, but the "abode of the true one" and "a garden of flowers where life is ever in bloom". Undoubtedly, it is transitory for an individual, but then, this is the only opportunity also for man "to meet his God" and to pull out all the weeds of evil, no matter where grown, in one's own consciousness or out of oneself, in this race or that and of whatever hue they are – social, moral, intellectual or political. The Sikh Gurus have used a number of religious terms to convey the sense of the highest state of bliss. The highest state of spiritual realisation, according to Sikhism, is not a negative state – it is not a state of void. In his discourse with many Buddhist and Hindu sages, Guru Nanak reinterpreted the meaning of the term "*sunya*" in a non-conventional way. According to him, sunya (silence eternal) is the power of the infinite. Mysticism (in both Sufism and Sikhism) talks about a transcendental form from *the lower self* to *the higher self* in the following way: For moving from Phenomenal to Noumenal, one must give up Ego.

Figure 2.6

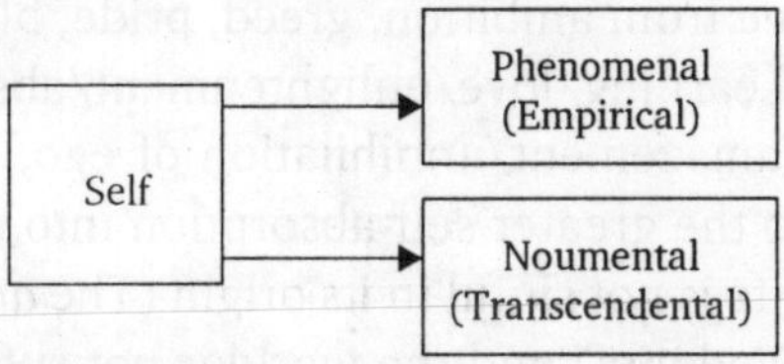

The Vedantic genius grasped long ago the truth that problems springing from secular pursuits cannot be resolved by inexorably pressing forward on the secular route. Equally clearly it was perceived that the answer to growing complexity is not to invite a greater or more bizarre tangle of complexity. The solution lay in the conjunction of their opposites: the sacred and the simple. This insight was formulated into a four-goal view (Chaturvarga) of human existence:

- *Dharma* – righteousness,
- *Artha* – money and wealth,
- *Kama* – fesired and needs, and
- *Moksha* – liberation of the spiritual core.

We must remember that the authentic Indian model of leadership has always been that of the *rajarshi*. Basically, *rajarshi* embodies the keynote of the Vedantic ethos: the management of the secular in the light of the sacred.

The summary of all four philosophical doctrines are given here to apply the basic postulates of these ideas in a broader sense:

Buddhism: Suffering/ignorance/ultimate goal/eight-fold path:

1. Complete view,
2. Complete aspiration,
3. Complete truthful speech,
4. Complete action,
5. Complete vocation,
6. Complete application,
7. Complete recollection, and
8. Complete contemplation.

Sufism: Free from ambition, greed, pride, blind obedience to custom, Learning/love/enlightenment/absorption/unity consciousness/amazement/annihilation of ego, the lower self and rebirth into the greater self-absorption into the unity.

Sikhism: Life is not sinful in its origin (The *amritasya putra* concept of the Vedanta) and the world is not suffering either.

Vedanta:

1. *Atmonomokshartha jagat dhitya cha:* has got two components, namely, self-emancipation and benefiting all in the world for real development,
2. *Tat tavm asi:* Everybody has immense potentiality
3. *Advaita:* Non-dual concept.

What role then has the Indian corporate sector to play in the world? The task is to make spirituality practical in every field. As Vivekananda said, with the advancement of science and technology, people are giving more importance to the so-called objective world and material pleasure. Unless we set a higher goal, material goals will prove to be detrimental to human civilisation.

We may observe some of the important aspects of teachings that have been enshrined in Buddhism (the ultimate goal and the eight-fold path to get rid of suffering and ignorance, i.e., from self-appraisal to self-reliance through the path of self-development), Sufism (to be free from ambition, greed, egotism, etc., enlightenment, absorption, unity consciousness et al. are to be cultivated as in the ABO model we suggest), Sikhism (wherein it has been highlighted that since we come from a holy source, we have to be holy through self-development) and Vedanta (*moksha* – the way forward is to become independent step by step, Advaita or the holistic approach that helps corporate executives move form self-centredness to collective responsibility and *shraddha*).

In Freudian psychology, behaviour is seen as the end-product of unknown forces hidden in the unconscious psyche. Conscious phenomena are governed by unconscious forces and polarities, which are irrational. As we know, Freud said that the topography of the human psyche comprises three distinct parts: id, ego and superego. Id is the primitive, instinctual root with its powerful biological programmes intended for survival. Superego is the moral conscience in the individual and is a socially fabricated product. The battle-ground where these two forces, id and superego, meet is ego.

The central issue relating to morality in man is whether he is capable of making the right choice among a basket of choices, all of which are individually and socially productive. Freud wanted us to believe that all the moral urges in man are the end result of an ongoing battle in him.

Kohlberg classifies the development of moral reasoning in man into three stages.[22] These are: (i) morality by fear in childhood, (ii) morality by social conformity and convention, and (iii) morality by internal conviction. Kohlberg reiterates that morality in man emerges through an internal cognitive reorganisation rather than through a simple acquisition of the moral concepts prevalent in a given culture.

Coping with stress, which is one of the major attributes of ethical dilemmas in the corporate context, is an internal experience in response to perceived stress. The single most powerful variable involved in stress tolerance is one's attitude to events. Attitude to life is the most significant "metaprogramme" in use and the impact of any external event on its use should be evaluated against this background. Our CAIA model also elucidates the same. Models of the world constructed within us are to a great extent the result of attitudes adopted. In this relation, a person reviews the outer events in relation to his interpretations and, in the process, he changes himself.

In the newly emerged post-industrial society, man has embarked upon a rat race, characterised by unhealthy competition, drive for supremacy and self-aggrandisement. Even, within the family, individuals live in mutually exclusive "mental boxes" and practise the art of mutual exploitation for selfish ends. A socio-centric milieu compels people to wear social masks and adopt socially prescribed roles, leading to hypocrisy and self-deceit.

The central core of one's being is the freedom to choose any path or pattern, but once the choice is made, the degree of central freedom is progressively curtailed from centre to periphery. At a later point of time, the person is drawn to the objective realities of his original choice. "What happens to a person is characteristic of him. He represents a pattern and all the pieces fit. One by one, as his life proceeds, they fall into place according to some predestined design" (Jung, 1955)

According to Horney, an individual's intrapsyschic life is culturally conditioned.[23] His internal value system and personal construct are knitted in accordance with the values of the society in which he lives. By assigning a greater role to environmental influence and learning process in the moulding of personality and behaviour, Horney has rejected "Freudian determinism". To Horney, psychotherapy means re-education and education of milieu, because his concept of "self" is a "dynamics self" that changes forever, with active attention, choice and responsibility.

Assagioli[24] conceptualises the nature of the "experiential self" in the following ways:

1. Lower consciousness, comprising the reflex functions of the body, i.e., instinct, drives, emotions and various automatic propensities demanding instant expression.
2. Middle Consciousness, corresponding to the Freudian "preconscious", the peripheral margin of our waking consciousness.

3. Consciousness with which we are aware of our immediate reality.
4. Our conscious self or the background of the flowing contents of consciousness.
5. Super consciousness, the region of self from where higher vision and aspirations originate,
6. The higher self, i.e., the centre of self from where higher vision and aspirations originate.
7. The collective unconscious: According to Assagioli, this means a membrane delimiting a cell, with a kind of "psychological osmosis" going on all the time both with other human beings and the general psychic environment.

Assagioli differentiates his "higher self" from Freud's superego and cautions us that the higher self should not be confused with the superego of Freud, which, according to him, is an artificial product.

Summarising the deliberations in our paper, we may now put forward that one must behave ethically in one's personal life to reflect positivity in corporate life. The concept of "critical behavioural positivity" will highlight its underlying importance only when we try to change our own mind-set first, then guard against the perception of threat that comes to us from mainly two sources: internal environment (within the family, society and organisation) and the external environment (uncontrollable situations that are alien such as global competition and technological revolution, the new world order etc). Self-centredness, therefore, becomes a defence mechanism, which puts us in a state of tamas (i.e., darkness, voidness or a static state). To pull us out of this quagmire, we have to try positively to build confidence, trust and fearlessness within ourselves, which bear a "trade-off" relationship with threat, which in most cases, is a perceived one and not real.

Thus, through rigorous practice of attitude control by any of the ways given by Buddhism, Sufism, Sikhism or the Vedanta (the Indian models) discussed herein, we can definitely reach a level of Being, Awareness and Bliss (Satchidananda), which demolishes the CAIA barrier and, as a corollary, there will be no compartmentalised attitude like controlled conscious behaviour in private and in corporate/ public life. The Indian model teaches us that each soul is potentially divine and the only thing that we have to do is to unveil the "darkness mask" thrown around us, which has conditioned us negatively and debarred us from making a move forward. The ABO approach, as discussed, is but a tool for achieving the "enlightened" level through *karmayoga* or work directedness.

Figure 2.7

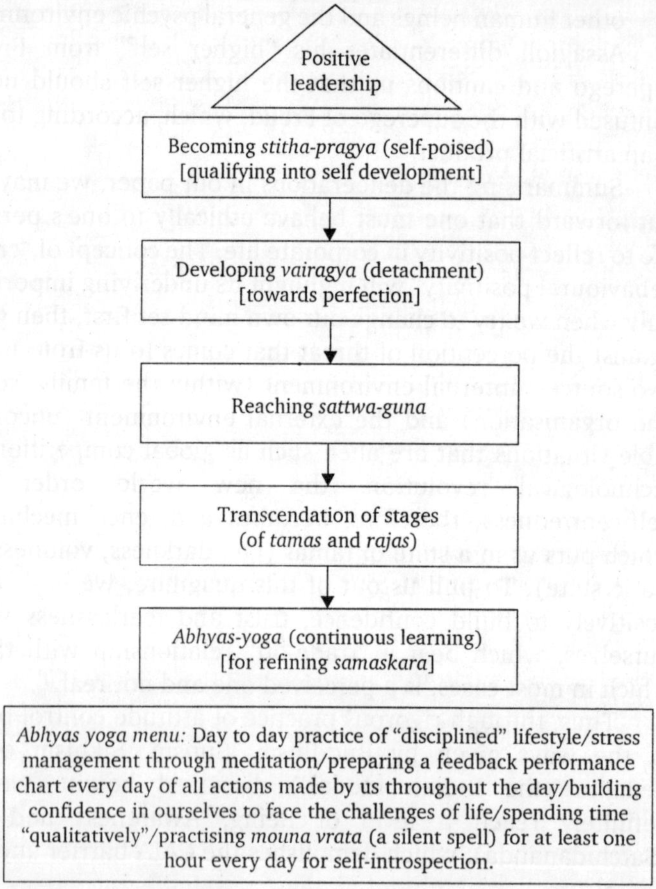

For transformational development with relation to the corporate sector, we formulate here a model (Figure 2.7), which leads to positive leadership with continuous learning methodology at the base. We are putting forward at the same time the menu for *abhyas-yoga* (continuous learning methodology)

Self-awareness at a higher level of "being" leads us accurately to the path of bliss or *ananda*. In an age of uncertainty, shocks and waves, we have to thrive in the right direction in order to save the world from perishing.

Notes

1. Immanuel Kant, "An Answer to the Question: What is Enlightenment?" *Kant's Political Writing*, Translated by H.B. Nisbet, Ed. Hans Reiss, Cambridge, Cambridge University Press, 1970.
2. John Rawls, *A Theory of Justice*, Cambridge, MA, Harvard University Press, 1971.
3. S. Sadri and Jayashree, *The Theory and Practice of Managerial Ethics*, Jaico, Mumbai, 1999.
4. Debraj Ray, *Development Economics*, OUP, 1998.
5. Amartya Sen, *On Ethics and Economics*, OUP, New Delhi, 1987.
6. Ibid.
7. Ibid.
8. Ibid.
9. H.B. Nisbet, Kant's Political Writing, (Trans.) Ed. Hans Reiss, Cambridge, 1970.
10. A.V. Miller, Hegel: Phenomonology of Spirit, (Trans.), Oxford, 1977.
11. Darryl Reed, "Corporate Social Responsibilities and Development in India," *Journal of Human Values,* 4:2,1998.
12. Ibid.
13. J. Habermas, *The Theory of Communicative Action*, Boston, 2 volumes, 1984, 1987. (As quoted in *From Modernism to*

Postmodernism: An Anthology, Ed. Lawrence Cahoone, Blackwell Publishers, Oxford, 1996, reprinted 1997).
14. Ibid.
15. Ibid.
16. Someswarananda, *Indian Wisdom for Management: A Textbook on Indian Management*, AMA, Ahmedabad, India, 1996.
17. Ibid.
18. Ibid.
19. Daniel W. Sherrick, "Corporate Restructuring: Perspective of Organized Labor", in the Center for Business Ethics at Bentley College, Ed. *The Ethics of Organizational Transformation: Mergers, Takeovers and Corporate Restructuring*, October 15 and 16, 1987, USA (as quoted in *Strategic Human Resource Management*: William P. Anthony, Pamela L. Perrewe and K. Michael Kacmar, 1993, The Dryden Press, Orlando, Florida, USA).
20. S.K. Chakraborty, *Management by Values: Towards a Cultural Congruence*, OUP, Mumbai, 1991.
21. Ananda Das Gupta, "Economic Management and Ethics: The Vedantic Answer", *Indian Journal of Public Administration*, New Delhi, July-September 1995.
22. L. Kohlberg, "Implications of Developmental Psychology for Education", *Educational Psychologist*, England, 1973.
23. K. Horney, "The Neurotic Personality of Our Time", New York, 1937 (as quoted in *Vedic Thought and Western Psychology* by Dr Shivaram Karikal, Arathi Publications, Mangalore, 1994).
24. Assagioli, as quoted in *Vedic Thought and Western Psychology* by Dr Shivram Karikal, Arathi Publications, Mangalore, 1994.

Note: For theories like deontology, teleology and praxis and some other ethics-related discussions, the author is mainly grateful to the works of Legge, 1998; Sadri et al., 1999; and Sen, 1987 (consult reference list for details).

3

Knowledge Management, Body Shopping and Frustrations: Search for Morality in the Post-modernist Era

The idea of different forms of knowledge was introduced by Nonaka and Takeuchi.[1] In their contributions, they introduced a number of concepts, one of the most important being the distinction between explicit and tacit knowledge. Explicit knowledge deals with manuals and procedures. Tacit knowledge, on the other hand, is learnt only though experience and communicated individually with the use of metaphors and analogy. In essence, tacit knowledge can be compared to a craftsman, who, after years of experience, has a wealth of expertise at his fingertips. Explicit knowledge can be processed by a computer or stored in a database. With some highly interesting case studies, the researchers illustrate how the "knowledge creation" theory has been successfully implemented in Japanese companies like Canon, Matsushita, Honda, etc.

Knowledge management is the process by which organisations generate wealth from intellectual assets. It is an emerging

Figure 3.1

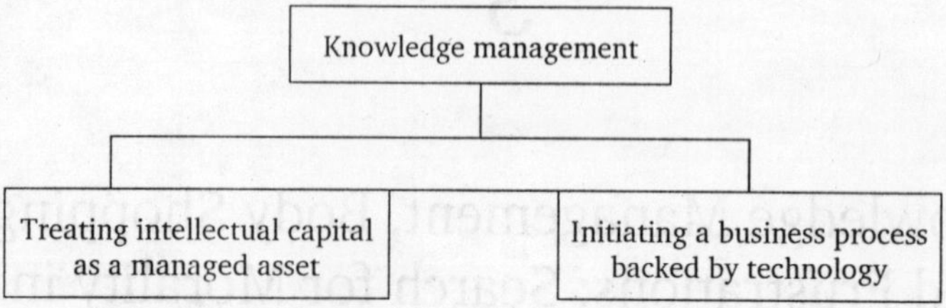

discipline that treats intellectual capital as a managed asset. It is also a business process backed by technology (Figure 3.1).

Knowledge management involves creating a process and a product by which otherwise unlinked departments can share information in order to improve service to internal or external customers and to ensure that the employees' effort is not duplicated. Knowledge management hinges upon the presumption that the workers in an organisation possess knowledge that can be converted into concrete business improvements if the information is harvested and disseminated to others to whom it could be of use. True knowledge management must involve capturing the internal knowledge generated by a firm – its best thinking on products, customers, competitors and processes – and sharing it.

It is also important to note that knowledge is no longer a long-term asset (Figure 3.2), which can be accumulated like cash reserves. Rather it is a perishable commodity that should be harvested from the talent within an organisation and harnessed by managers who must always be on the lookout for it.

Knowledge repositories occupy a central place in any knowledge management system (KMS). A knowledge repository is an online, computer-based storehouse of original information, expertise, experience and documents about a particular domain of knowledge. As Rastogi[2] elaborated: "Creation of a knowledge repository involves collection, summarisation, organisation and integration of knowledge

Figure 3.2

A Complete Lifecycle for Knowledge Management

1. Capture of knowledge from external and internal sources
2. Classification of knowledge according to managerial and technical necessities
3. Valuation of knowledge
4. Access of knowledge
5. Use of knowledge
6. Improvement of knowledge
7. Retirement of knowledge when it has outlived its usefulness

across multiple information sources. It serves as a foundation and knowledge source that supports problem solving, performance improvement, skills and capability development and process reengineering efforts."

Rastogi further says: "Innovation or innovativeness (I), competencies and capabilities (C&C), streamlined processes (SP), human capital (HC) and knowledge management system (KMS) of an organisation conjoin together to create its intellectual capital (IC). The latter, in turn, strengthens the firm's strategy (CS) and influences its business environment (BE)."[3]

While the IT industry, primarily a knowledge industry, has been in the forefront in following knowledge management, others like pharmaceuticals, manufacturing, R&D organisations, petrochemicals, etc., are catching up fast. If Infosys has a companywide intranet, called Sprash, akin to a central information portal, Wipro Technologies has created virtual communities for employees with common interests to share views and experiences.

Whither Knowledge Workers?

Looking at the examples from well-known companies like Hitachi, Toshiba and Intel given below, we find the so-called knowledge workers are facing the threat of losing jobs in bulk or that some of them have already been fired against the euphoric concept of knowledge management, which basically advocates sharing, applying and creating:

Example 1: Japanese electronics giant Hitachi Ltd decided to cut 14,700 jobs or 4 per cent of its global workforce and post a $1.2 billion group net loss from the middle of 2001 to March 2002. Of the total, 10,200 jobs would be cut in Japan and the remaining 4,500 from overseas operations. Hitachi has become the latest victim of the global technology industry slowdown.

Example 2: Joining a growing list of Japanese manufacturers forced to cut jobs amid a global IT downturn, Toshiba Corp. slashed 17,000, or about 9 per cent of its worldwide workforce, in three years starting from the middle of 2001.

Example 3: Chipmaker Intel Corp. lowered revenue estimates for the first quarter in 2001 by about 25 per cent and said it would cut its workforce by 6 per cent, or 5,000 jobs, mainly through attrition.

Recently, a survey was conducted in India among 150 knowledge workers who revealed that as many as 70 per cent were not really keen to rejoin the company they were working for, while 27 per cent were definite that they could not rejoin the company they were working for.[4] While 27 per cent were definite they would not, 43 per cent said they probably would not. Only 1 per cent was absolutely certain it would opt for the current employer again.

Overall, while 54 per cent of the employees covered said they were satisfied with their employer, only 2 per cent said they were extremely satisfied. Among the dissatisfied, 25 per cent slotted themselves as somewhat dissatisfied and 3 per cent chose to call themselves very dissatisfied. Predictably, with knowledge workers being fairly well-paid, compensation was not a major factor for dissatisfaction. (Figure 3.3)

Figure 3.3

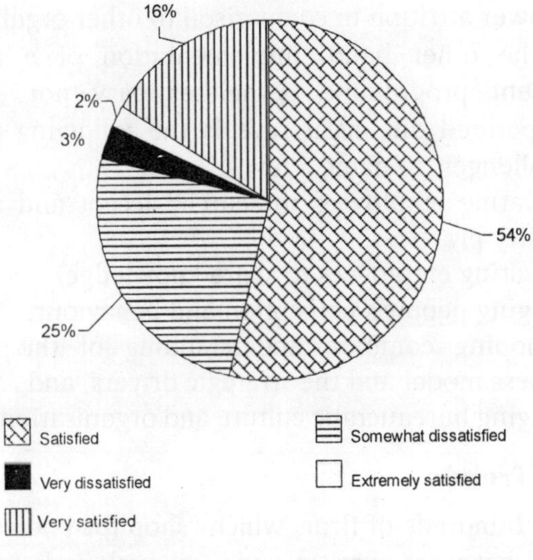

Source: NFO-MBL Survey, 2001.

In fact, this study lists the top five factors for dissatisfaction among knowledge workers as:

1. Job content,
2. Interpersonal relations,
3. Work climate,
4. Training and Development, and
5. Communication.

In terms of importance, job content scored as high as 86 per cent. Work climate followed with 83 per cent, quality work practices with 82 per cent, communication with 78 per cent and interpersonal relations with 74 per cent.

Covering the age group between twenty and thirty years plus and work experience ranging between two and over nine years, the study also found that dissatisfaction among older employees was higher than among younger employees.

Dissatisfaction also increased with the tenure of experience. While employees with over nine years of experience again put satisfaction levels at 0 per cent, those with two-five years of experience put it at 21 per cent.

The study observes that "value-driven organisations witness lower attrition in comparison to other organisations".

On the other hand, implementation of a knowledge management programme is neither easy nor simple, as Rastogi[5] pointed out, as it reveals the following implementation challenges, to name a few:

1. Motivating employees to search, accept and adopt best industry practices,
2. Motivating employees to share knowledge,
3. Changing people's perception and behaviour,
4. Developing common understanding of the company's business model and the strategic drivers, and
5. Changing bureaucratic culture and organisation structure.

Current Trends

There are hundreds of firms which "shop for bodies". In such cases, the software worker ends up exploited, in terms of working hours if not in terms of salary. Indian software professionals working abroad often work five-ten more hours than their western counterparts. Such firms are often one-man Indian ventures in Noida or Gurgaon, but they can also be multinational consultancy firms such as Pricewaterhouse-Coopers. This firm keeps a stock of workers that it sends out on different projects, without actually having a software development centre itself.

Several young recruits surveyed, however, were quite definite about their plans. They would surely take up a foreign offer, save money and then come back to India to set up their own companies. They were going by the example set by their peers. Such workers might perhaps regard any exploitation as a necessary evil to achieve their goal.

The fate of people trained in one of the myriad training institutes mushrooming all over the country is much less certain. They are likely to end up being body-shopped for data entry work, with considerably less pay than their formally trained counterparts.

According to industry surveys, the IT sector grew by around 33 per cent in 1998-99, from Rs 18,015 crore in 1997-98 to Rs 23,955 crore. Of this, the domestic sector grew at 21.8 per cent, while the export segment grew by around 60 per cent to cross the Rs 10,000 crore mark. However, in the hardware market, growth was actually negative in value-of-sales terms, mainly due to the fall in prices of personal computers, and a severe depression in the workstation market. In the uncertain political scenario of the latter half of 2001, neither government departments nor large industrial houses were willing to invest in new equipment till a stable government was in place.

II
Post-modern Organisations

In so far as organisations are concerned, including "knowledge organisations", we find that post-modernists argue that one view that has been inappropriately privileged is that of the *organisation,* rather than the *process* of organising. They say that an organisation is not one thing but many and these do not have clearly defined insides and outsides, and because the boundaries are uncertain and reversible, no organisation, no description of it can ever be complete.

Figure 3.4

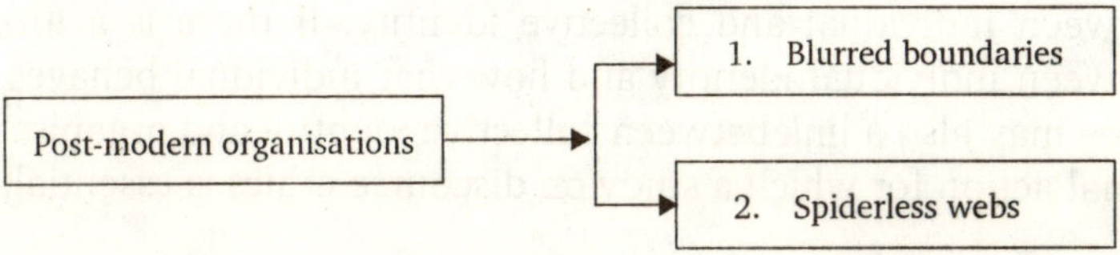

The characteristics of post-modern organisations can be viewed in Figure 3.4.

Post-modernists say that organisations have blurred boundaries because they are far from fixed as traditionally distinctive organisational boundaries that "separate" a particular organisation from other organisations are becoming increasingly fluid and transient.

About organisations becoming spiderless webs, post-modernists argue that everyone is enmeshed in the practices, procedures, rules and regulations that comprise an organisation because of the pervasive effect of history and society. The web of power works on the body as well as the mind.

Thus, the post-modernist approach reminds us of the fragmentary and multiple nature of an organisation's identity that has a number of implications for our understanding of and work in it:

First, we should see people *in* the organisation rather than *of* the organisation because an organisation carries only some parts of the individual and often recognises only particular "taken for granted" aspects – age, service, job classification; the individual's other facets are ignored by the organisational bureaucracy.

Second, our organisational identities cannot be divorced from our non-work identities.

Third, post-modern approaches draw attention to the irrelevance of cutting up the world into distinctions that may no longer be meaningful. So, for example, as the practices associated with empowerment become more widespread, there is more self and peer management to be found in organisations.

Finally, post-modernism draws our attention to the link between individual and collective identity. If there is a link between individual identity and how that individual behaves, there may also a link between collective identity and organisational action for which a study on discourse ethics is essential.

III
Discourse Ethics: A Tool for Common Dialoguing

Doing the right thing, particularly in organisational settings, requires people to seek solutions together.

The approach does not try to set out the conditions that make an act ethical (because it is virtuous, utilitarian or whatever); rather, this approach sets out a procedure for arriving at ethical conclusions based on reasoned agreement among concerned participants. The approach is called discourse ethics (championed by Jürgen Habermas).[6]

Conversations on moral issues allow understanding of ethical norms to be developed and shared, whether in organisations or in society generally. Ethics is not about meeting an external criterion, but about people learning from one another. Such conversations have obvious characteristics – participants must be sincere, respect each other's views, be fair in examining each other's positions, and be accountable in seeking to question and be questioned. These characteristics of good conversations – sincerity, respect, fairness and accountability – are also frequently cited as traits of good solutions to workplace dilemmas, and of course as values of ethical organisations.

Habermas is widely considered as the most influential thinker in Germany over the past decade (1980-90). As a philosopher and sociologist, he has mastered and creatively articulated an extraordinary range of specialised literature in the social sciences, social theory and the history of ideas in the provocative critical theory of knowledge and human interests.

Habermas differentiates three primary generic cognitive areas in which human interest generates knowledge. These areas determine categories relevant to what we interpret as knowledge. In today's modern management realm, knowledge management has carved a niche for itself and that is the reason why Habermas is gaining a prominent place even in the literature of management. That is, why they are termed "knowledge constitutive" – they determine the mode of discovering knowledge and whether knowledge claims can be

Figure 3.5

Habermas' Three Domains of Knowledge

• Type of human interest	• Kind of knowledge	• Research methods
• Technical (prediction)	• Instrumental (causal explanation)	• Positivistic sciences (empirical-analytic methods)
• Practical (interpretation and understanding)	• Practical (understanding)	• Interpretive Research (hermeneutic methods)
• Emancipatory (criticism and liberation)	• Emancipation (reflection)	• Critical social sciences (critical theory methods)

warranted. These areas define cognitive interests or learning domains, and are grounded in different aspects of social existence – work, interaction and power (Figure 3.5).

Work Knowledge

Work broadly refers to the way one controls and manipulates one's environment. This is commonly known as instrumental action Knowledge is based upon empirical investigation and governed by technical rules. The criterion of effective control of reality direct what is or is not appropriate action. Empirical-analytic sciences using hypothetical-deductive theories characterise this domain. Much of what we consider "scientific" research domains, for example, physics, chemistry and biology are classified by Habermas as belonging to the domain of work.

Practical Knowledge

The practical domain identifies human social interaction or "communicative action". Social knowledge is governed by binding consensual norms which define reciprocal expectations about behaviour between individuals. Social norms can be related to empirical or analytical propositions, but their validity is grounded "only in the intersubjectivity of the mutual understanding of intentions". The criterion of clarification of conditions for communication and intersubjectivity (the understanding of meaning rather than causality) is used to determine what is appropriate action. Many of the historical-hermeneutic disciplines – descriptive social science, history, aesthetics, law, ethnographic literature and so on are classified by Habermas as belonging to the domain of the practical.

Emancipatory Knowledge

The emancipatory domain identifies self-knowledge' or "self-reflection". This involves interest in the way one's history and biography has expressed itself, in the way one sees oneself, one's roles and social expectations. Emancipation is from libidinal, institutional or environmental forces which limit our options and rational control over our lives, but have been taken for granted as beyond human control (also known as "reification"). Insights gained through critical self-awareness are emancipatory in the sense that at least one can recognise the correct reasons for one's problems. Knowledge is gained by self-emancipation through reflection leading to a transformed consciousness or "perspective transformation". Examples of critical sciences include feminist theory, psychoanalysis and the critique of ideology, according to Habermas.

In what respect does discourse ethics contain meta ethical – that is, propaedeutic – elements? The answer is initially easy: Meta-ethical reflections are a part of discourse ethics in defining what is a moral question and what is not. Beyond the embeddedness of discourse ethics in the development of western rationality and in the process of differentiation of rationality (in its three types of theoretical, practical and expressive rationality), it is a meta-ethical framework in a broad sense. Habermas chooses a specific way of combining theoretical meta-ethical statements with the practical world, the "life world" contexts (*lebensweltlichen Kontexten*), in his discourse ethics. From this point of view, discourse ethics is neither pure meta-ethics nor applied ethics. It undertakes to combine the claim of universality that is inherent theoretical knowledge with a theory of moral practice. And it even claims to conjoin the sphere of theoretical justification of the theory with the sphere of practice.

One point in question in Habermas' discourse ethics is the relation between empirical foundation and transcendental method, between context orientation und decontextualisation in the so-called "moral point of view", which is the phrase Habermas uses to describe the specific dimension of morality, i.e., normative questions.

Cognitivism

Discourse ethics starts from the assumption that moral problems are capable of being solved in a rational and cognitive way. This is against a moral scepticism which asserts that questions of practical reason cannot be decided on rational grounds: "Non-cognitivistic conceptions are reducing the value of the whole world of moral intuitions based in every day life".[7] With this confession to a cognitivism in moral theory, however, Habermas does not intend to assimilate the specific phenomenon of "morality" to what is the domain of cognitivism, i.e., "truth."

To say it in analytic terms: Normative sentences cannot be treated as propositions or as assertive sentences. There is obvious difference between "You ought not kill" and "This grass is green". Hence, the term "moral truth" is quite a difficult one, as Habermas himself recognises.

Second, Habermas situates the validity claim of normative sentences in a social-evolutionary context: The differentiation of the validity claims of normative justification and of truth is the result of the process of modernisation. Discourse ethics is a normative ethics for pluralistic societies which no longer have a single, overarching moral authority.

Justice vs good: Another second basic decision results from the cognitivistic theory of ethics: Questions of morality are defined as questions of justifying norms. The mediating structure of "substantive ethics" (*sittlichkeit*), which is crucial to Hegel's central critique of Kant's moral theory, is in Habermas' theory only important for particular forms of life (*lebensformen*) and contexts. In his conception of the "life-world" *lebenswelt,* Habermas has worked out the limitedness (*begrenztheit*) of this horizon – a limitedness which is culturally, historically and socially mediated and within which takes place the substantial determination of our imaginations and aims to fulfil individually our "good life". The phenomenal domain of morality, as Habermas understands it, is in his view structured by inter-subjectivity quite different from the phenomenal domain of substantive ethics (*sittlichkeit*). The "moral point of view" has a force to transcend the particularity of the contexts. We are entering the sphere of morality when we are in conflict with others, when there is conflict and dissent (*dissens*). Moral theory has the task of preparing our means of responding (*instrumentarium*) to a partial destruction of the "life-world" (*lebenswelt*). Moral theory provides a sort of mending or repair. Thus, Habermas differentiates strictly between "questions of the good life" and "questions of justice". (In this direction lies also the difference between "norms" and "values".) This is quite plausible because determining what a "good life" is, under conditions of value pluralism, has to be necessarily a limited determination. For that reason, Habermas emphasises the role of a formal moral theory, such as discourse ethics, in creating the space needed for a pluralism of many different "good lives".

But certainly moral questions arise in the context of the "life-world", where our beliefs and decisions are shaped by values, habits and prejudices. Here reappears the problem: To what degree, on the one hand, must moral theory transcend the particularity of the life-world so as to ensure impartiality and justice, without, on the other hand, being so general and universal that it is no longer relevant as a criterion for moral conflicts?

Universalisation

The essential point of discourse ethics by Habermas is formulated in the "principle of universalisation" and what it entails – namely, the "principle of discourse". Habermas reformulates the Kantian version of the principle of universalisation in terms of inter-subjectivity. The principle of universalisation explains what our every-day, but post-conventional intuition would outline for us as a strategy for solving moral conflicts: the "principle of impartiality".

Habermas insists on the principle of impartiality, which constitutes a formal framework for both different mores and acts of solidarity.

Concomitantly, the principle of universalisation (U) is formally stated as follows: A norm is valid only if "all affected can accept the consequences and the side-effects its general observance can be anticipated to have for the satisfaction for everyone's interests (and these consequences are preferred to those of known alternative possibilities)".[8] In this way, the principle of universalisation formally determines those conditions which must be met if the claim of legitimacy – the claim advanced by moral commands and norms – is really justified.

IV

On having a consideration for the implications of knowledge management first, then the actual situation and working culture in which the knowledge workers are, where lies our individual identity and its functional relationship with the collective identity?

Looking thus into the ethical dimensions of knowledge management, we may put forward a few models which post-modern organisations may take as a prescription for putting their organisations on the right path.

Based on the principles of management theory, four factors are identified here to develop the work culture in an organisation:

1. Vision and mission:
   a. Company value,
   b. Customer orientation,
   c. Quality standard, and
   d. Productivity norms.
2. Values:
   a. Welfare and promotional yardsticks, and
   b. Brand building and sustenance.
3. Strategy:
   a. Training process,
   b. Leadership and motivation, and
   c. R&D initiatives.

Now, obviously, the question arises: How should the key factors, namely vision, mission, values and strategy, conducive to the enhancement of work culture development be implemented in an organisation?

These factors are basically holistic in nature and use the SEWA (self-mastery, empathy for all, worker directedness and achievement in performance) approach in their application. Together, they constitute "action by objective (AB), a concept that is already being discussed to provide a broad understanding of a "positive" organisation, which has developed a "positive" work culture fully.

The concept of ABO is based on five principles:

1. Caring for others,
2. Helping them to solve problems,
3. This makes the team morally driven,
4. The team becomes more independent, and
5. This leads the team to self-realisation.

Thus, ABO team members are those who:

1. Produce performers,
2. Set personal examples; visible accessible on the move,
3. Find ways to overcome obstacles, and
4. Manage them.

Therefore, with the technique of ABO, the work culture in an organisation can be pointed towards the harmonisation paradigm, which embraces two aspects:

1. Immediate goal achievement factors, and
2. Ultimate goal achievement factors.

The immediate goal achievement factors comprise:

(a) Direction setting,
(b) Resolution of conflicts, and
(c) Team spirit.

These three factors culminate in ultimate goal achievement, i.e., self-reliance – the centre of the halo from which the following four result-oriented factors are diffused:

1. Knowledge based performance,
2. Value-based management,
3. Development forward excellence, and
4. Shared goals.

The four components of the SEWA model (self mastery, empathy for all, worker directedness and achievement in performance) are aimed at a "positively reinforced" mission, which includes:

1. Involvement of people	Creating opportunities
2. Innovation and growth	Building up the future
3. Developing positive leadership	Strategic edging
4. Creating "positive" teams in the following directions:	
(a) Operating team	Plan and execute, charting out the method of "focussed" work
(b) Facilitator team	Day to day management
(c) Vision team	Coping with the changes and steps to be taken accordingly

The "focussed" work mentioned as a function of the operating team may be explained through a flow-chart (Figure 3.6).

This process of "self-evaluation" and thinking along a new dimension will lead to value-addition by the managers and organisations on a common-sharing basis.

Figure 3.6

"Focussed" Work

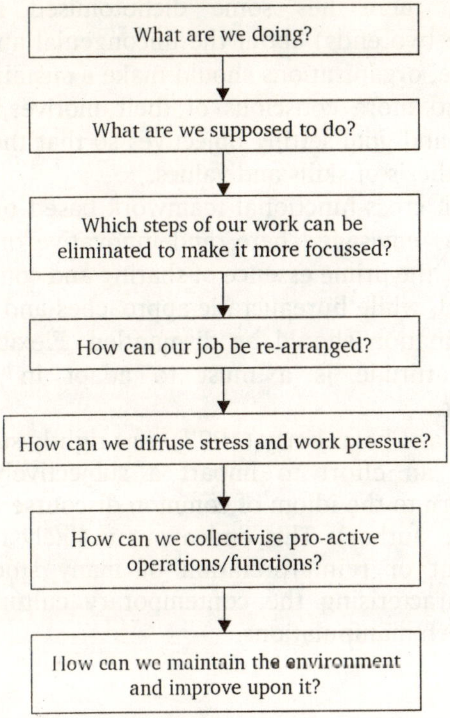

The key components of the new paradigm are vision lending much-needed boundaries to organisations to evolve values and beliefs deeply implemented in the organisational culture and simultaneously inculcating values in the knowledge workers. There should be symbiosis among the four essential factors: assimilation and embracement, emphasis on higher meaning, austerity and simplicity and, above all, divinity.

For practising a value-driven environment in the knowledge management sector, which is ridden with uncertainty about the future, about job security, about job content (as most IT companies thrive on "imported" time-bound projects), about strained interpersonal relationships (since most of the vertical promotional avenues of knowledge workers depend mainly on the appraisal reports of the HR department, there lies some dichotomised relationships between the two ends) about the uncongenial and cut-throat work climate, organisations should make a sustained effort to be more and more conscious of their motives, tendencies, preferences and goal-setting objectives so that there can be a positive synthesis of skills and values.

Through cross-functional teamwork based on the SEWA principles, as envisaged here, and innovative organisational mechanisms, the prime essence of sharing and conviction must be facilitated, while bureaucratic approaches and hierarchical power domination should be dismantled. Flexibility with a "focussed" attitude is a must to adapt in a changing environment.

In sum, as Chakraborty (1997)[9] has rightly suggested, we must make an effort to impart a subjectively pure and authentic turn to the idiom of common discourse (emphasis is given by the author). This endeavour is likely to entail the abandonment or reinterpretation of many stock objective phrases characterising the contemporary culture of bewildering sci-tech manipulations.

Notes

1. T. Nonaka and Takeuchi, *The Knowledge Creating Companies: How Japanese Companies Create the Dynamics of Innovation*, Oxford University Press, London, 1995.
2. P. N. Rastogi, "Dynamics of Knowledge Management & Intellectual Capital" (New Delhi, *Productivity*, Vol. 41, No. 4, January-March 2001.
3. NFO-MBL Report, As quoted in an article in *The Times of India*, Bangalore, August 22, 2001.
4. Rastogi, op. cit.
5. Rastogi, op. cit.
6. Jürgen Habermas, *Moral Consciousness and Communicative Action*, (Cambridge, MA, MIT Press, 1990), 62.

7. Jürgen Habermas, *Discourse Ethics: Notes on a Program of Philosophical Justification,* (Cambridge, MA, MIT Press, 1990), 65.
8. Jürgen Habermas, op. cit.
9. S.K. Chakraborty, 'Rising Technology and Falling Ethics', *Journal of Human Values*, 1997, 3(1), 103-18.

4

Management of the Changing Order: Some Ethical Dimensions

Since developing countries like India are seriously affected by a chronic productivity crisis, high incidence of industrial sickness, poor corporate financial results and unfavourable balance of payments, there is an urgent need for adopting human resource management (HRM) practices.

Schuster[1] confirms, through a "validity study" involving 460 large US industrial and 138 non-industrial companies that there exists a statistically significant relationship between practices and superior financial performance. Morita[2] also reveals that the secret of the extraordinary business success of Japanese corporations lies in their ability to create family like feelings among employees.

Based on these case studies and observations made by Schuster and Morita, Figure 4.1 shows the trend of modern management philosophy, which seeks to integrate individual needs and organisational needs into a composite set of unified goals (Das Gupta, 1996).[3]

The thrust of modern management philosophy is that it tends to believe in the genius of the "whole man" and tries to become more and more employee-centred, rather than

Figure 4.1

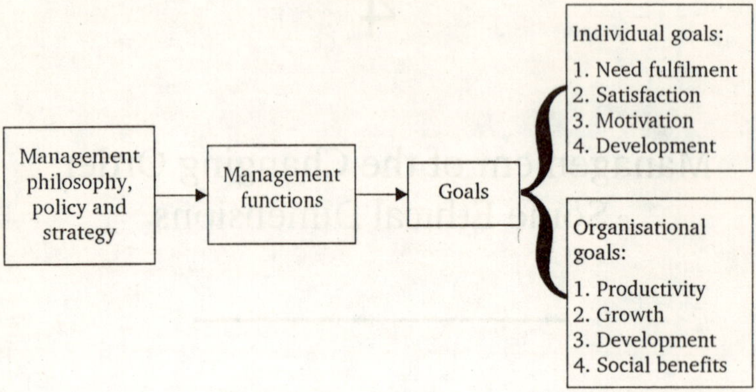

production-centred. The change is reflected in the progressive adoption of techniques in modern organisations. Many companies now follow what is called a 360-degree evaluation, where the assessment and the consequent emoluments are based on not only the appraisal of one's boss, but also that of one's peers and juniors. With the emphasis being on helping employees to achieve their full potential, especially as team players, it is only natural that companies should exercise equal care in selecting personnel. One technique to do this is the Myeres Bringgs Type Indicator (MBTI). This well-developed psychometric technique involves determining and typifying the applicant's personality into one of eight well-defined personality types making the selecting process much more scientific and less open to bias. Modi Xerox, Usha International etc. used MBTI in recent times for developing leadership qualities among their managers by stressing and developing individual personality traits. Another model is the Hay Model (HM), where the evaluation is based on the individual's knowledge base, problem solving ability and his accountability to the organisation. Eicher, Ford and New Holland have used the HM model for organisational development.

From the structural point of view, the anatomy of HRM consists of four basic components – acquisition, development,

Figure 4.2

Anatomy of HM: An Integrated View

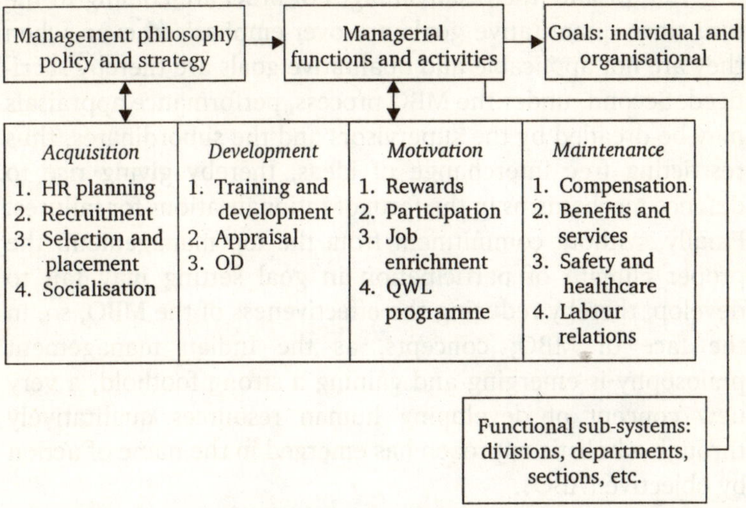

motivation and maintenance of employees. In Figure 4.2, we present a chart elaborating the four elements of HRM.

Crisis of leadership can be solved through a growth which is directed towards fulfilling social needs. There is a need for a "bottom-up" approach in the leadership, involving people right from the lowest level. A participative (neither autocratic nor free reign) leadership will necessarily be able to grow through direction (stage 2) to solve the crisis of mobility in the organisational milieu. Through a broad-based approach, growth through coordination will be possible (stage 4) with a back-up of more empowerment in the hands of the workforce (through *kaizen* small group activity, quality circles, etc.) to solve problems (stage 3). The crisis of vision of decision-makers can be solved by striking a balance between the "ego" (organisational needs) and "eco" (individual and social needs) (Das Gupta, 1993, 1995).[4]

For organisational development and human resources management, Peter Drucker has developed a philosophy, management by objective (MBO), which has four steps: (i) setting objectives (ii) developing an action plan (iii) conducting periodic reviews; and (iv) appraising performance.

But, of late, the disadvantages of MBO are coming to the fore since quantitative goals are over-emphasised even when they are not applicable and qualitative goals are thereby sacrificed. Second, under the MBO process, performance appraisals may be dreaded by the supervisors and the subordinates, thus restricting free interchange of ideas, thereby giving rise to defence mechanisms in the form of rationalisations for failures. Finally, without commitment from the top management, the proper climate of participation in goal setting may fail to develop, thereby reducing the effectiveness of the MBO, so, in the face of MBO; concepts, as the Indian management philosophy is emerging and gaining a strong foothold, a very new concept of developing human resources qualitatively through a holistic approach has emerged in the name of action by objective (ABO).

The entire human resources development scheme, if enshrined in the Indian context without adopting photocopied theories from western texts, will yield fruitful results as the crises in business are spiritual. The spirituo-technical approach makes a fundamental shift from the current reductionist ("lean-manufacturing" and other concepts of the West, emphasising lower costs, faster production, etc.), fragmentist, materialist paradigm to one which recognises relationships, consciousness and spirit as the right approach Peter Drucker admits with rare frankness that although he has tried to see the new dimensions of modern management, he has not been able to deal either with the moral horror or the spiritual agonies arising out of modern management culture.

There lies only one truth. If we want to develop human resources through a quality-oriented strategy, there is a requirement for a paradigm shift. The ABO model may prove to be a better alternative process with which to solve the "psycho-material" problem, if applied in a wider context in the Indian management arena.

Figure 4.3

Decision Style Model (based on Vedantic ideas of human nature)

Characters/ 30 traits	*Karma* (work-oriented)	*Jnana* (logistic)	*Yoga* (supra-conscious/ visionary)	*Bhakti* (feeling oriented)
Defining characteristics	Implementor	Analytical	Imaginator	Collaborator
Mindset	Pragmatic	Rationally oriented	Creative	Emotive
Inclination	Practical methods to act	Data, figures, charts, models	Alternatives	Informal meetings
Motivation	Practical approach	Intellectual approach	New ideas	Emotional approach
Dislikes	Vague ideas	Mental pictures	Details	Non-human factors

Someswarananda[5] prepared a model of decision styles based on the Vedantic ideas of human nature (Figure 4.3). According to his model, managers display the following orientations of *karma*, *jnana*, *yoga* or *bhakti*:

1. A *karma*-oriented manager is a no-nonsense person, he is organised.
2. A *jnana*-oriented manager is basically an analyser, always asking for logic, facts and figures.
3. A *yoga*-oriented manager is very creative, always bubbling with new ideas and always on the move.
4. A *bhakti*-oriented manager gives importance to feelings.

Someswarananda points out that managers with *karma* and *jnana* styles think that the intellect is more important, but managers with *yoga* and *bhakti* styles think that it is the feeling that is more important. Metaphorically, the *karma* style is represented by the "hand", i.e., action; *jnana* is represented by the "head", i.e., intellect; and *bhakti* is represented by the "heart", i.e., emotion.

On the other hand, the consciousness approach to management denotes that there is direct correspondence between man's inner life of thoughts, feelings and emotions – his consciousness – and the circumstances and events in his outer environment. The external situation is an extension of his inner consciousness expressed in outer life. This principle is derived from the most universally accepted spiritual knowledge "the truth of oneness".

In this context, Japan's corporate giant Matsushita's management philosophy may be taken into consideration as an

Figure 4.4

Performance Appraisals: Common Management Responsibilities

Planning	Develops and implements effective plans. Plans include long-range considerations. Establishment of quantitative/ qualitative work goals.
Organisation	Organises staff consistent with a thorough understanding of job responsibilities and effects change.
Decision	Accepts responsibility for making decisions. Qualifies decisions by considering all points of view.
Human resource development	Provides for subordinate training, HR planning and career development. Subordinates' developmental needs are specifically documented.

Missing Areas as Envisaged in ABO		
a.	Treatment programmes	
b.	Action-by-objective plans	Shared vision building Systematic thinking Dialogue and integration of diverse views ("mental models") Empowering people and inspiring commitments "Consciousness approach" Designing learning process
c.	Periodic review	

important one. It believes that the inherent preference of organisations is clarity, certainty and perfection. The inherent nature of human relationships involves ambiguity, uncertainty and imperfections. How one honours, balances and integrates the needs of both is the key to management.

The western model of performance appraisals through common management responsibilities (CMR) has earmarked different functional areas for focussing on evaluation (Figure 4.4). As a propagator of Indian management, we may discover a few weak points in the model. These include:

1. Absence of "treatment programmes",
2. "Action by objective plans" have been ignored, and
3. Importance has not been given to periodic reviews.

Thus, along with the components mentioned in CMR, we may develop the model. To start with, the treatment programmes should be divided into four segments:

1. For the rank and file level,
2. For the supervisory level,
3. For the management level, and
4. For all levels.

Segments rearranged, the main emphasis should now be on:

1. defining the role of the organisation,
2. setting goals, both particular and general (particular goal means the objectives of various departments/units which will ultimately culminate in the general goal and general goal means the main aim for achievement by the organisation),
3. pointing out the focus, i.e., the gap between the mission and the general goal, and
4. finding out various solutions to bridge the gap.

The treatment programme involves all the people of the organisation regarding how the goal can be achieved or the gap bridged through self-management teams (SMTs) in various units (Figure 4.4) as against the western HR strategy model, which ultimately stresses individual achievement

Figure 4.5

Self-management Team	
Tat Tam Asi	Self-confidence
Atmonomokartha jagatditaya cha	Understanding
Jnan/bhakti/yoga/karma	Man placement
Paraspara bhaabayanta	Team spirit
Karmashu kaushalam	Excellence in work
Moksha	Empowering

rather than group achievement – a crucial factor that has been underlined in our SMT model. The SMT model encompasses autonomy (*mukti*) and creative joy (*ananda*), which motivate people more than anything else. So, SMT can produce better results (Figure 4.5).

Secondly, ABO plans focus on team-building, for which shared vision building, systematic thinking, building "mental models" empowering people and inspiring commitment, enabling better and positive results are to be established and augmented through "designing a learning process" and the consciousness approach. At this point, we may give the example of an empirical study made by Khandwalla[6], which

Figure 4.6

Self-management Teams: A Comparative Table	
Khandwalla's study	ABO model
Commitment to innovation and experimentation	Components of ABO approach
Review and evaluation of project, including mid-course correction	Treatment programmes
Avoiding functional myopia	Vision through SMT
Active interest of management in sensing problems at operational level	Components of ABO approach
Obtaining ideas from lower level staff and encouraging them to participate	Building of SMT spirit

revealed a number of factors similar to those of ours, which contribute to the organisational learning process. This is being given on a comparative scale in Figure 4.6.

Thirdly, the periodic review of training programmes in our model consists of:

1. Reaction of participants, i.e., their response towards the programme and beyond that,
2. Learning, i.e., participants' intellectual assimilation of the concepts, ideas and principles of the training programme,
3. Behaviour changes, i.e., whether the training caused people to alter their behaviour on the job,
4. Impact of organisational effectiveness, i.e., whether the modified behaviour caused positive results, and
5. Subjective and objective criteria, i.e., subjective criteria call for the opinion of participants and objective criteria relate to the effects of training by measuring specific outcomes.

Finally, the model results in three "immediate goal achievement" factors:

1. Direction setting,
2. Resolution of conflicts, and
3. Team spirit.

This further culminate in "ultimate goal achievement", i.e., self-reliance from which the following four result oriented factors are diffused:

1. Knowledge based performance,
2. Value-based management,
3. Development forward excellence, and
4. Shared goals.

The ABO approach in management with all its ethical notes and value-orientation thus seeks to help organisations grow in an environment which could be conductive for Indian management philosophy. ABO, on the other hand, with all its components such as SMT, ABO plans, treatment programmes, etc., has its global aspect and this theory is able to the contribute to three major strategic factors that are essential in a competitive world:

1. The creation of "critical capabilities",
2. The fostering of "core competence", and
3. Building up of "knowledge creation".

Hayes and Pisano[7] have observed that traditionally, companies have viewed investments in new facilities, technology and R&D as the primary means to enhance their existing manufacturing capabilities. But according to the new approach to manufacturing strategy, managers should think about investments more in terms of their capacity to build new capabilities. Capabilities that provide enduring sources of competitive advantage are usually built over time through a series of investments in facilities, human capital and knowledge. A company's capabilities are more than its physical assets. In fact, they are largely embodied in the collective skills and knowledge of its people and the organisational procedures that shape the way employees interact.

Prahalad and Hamel[8] concluded that in the long-run competitiveness derives from an ability to build, at lower cost and more speedily than competitors, a well- integrated complex of production skills and streams of technologies, collectively called "core competencies", in a company. First, a core competence provides potential access to a wide variety of new and emerging markets. Second, a core competence should make a significant contribution to the perceived customer benefits of the product. Finally, a core competence should be difficult for competitors to imitate. And it will be difficult if it is a complex harmonisation of individual technologies and production skills. A rival might acquire some of the technologies and production skills that comprise the core competence, but to duplicate the comprehensive pattern of internal coordination and learning is not an easy task.

Nonaka and Takeuchi (1995) stress the need for two elements, viz., explicit knowledge and tacit knowledge, for building up knowledge. Explicit knowledge deals usually with manuals and procedures. Tacit knowledge, on the other hand, is learnt only through experience and communicated individually with the use of metaphors and analogy. In essence, tacit knowledge can be compared to a craftsman who, after years of experience, has a wealth of expertise at his fingertips. Explicit knowledge can be processed by a computer or stored in a database.

Finally, we observe that for building the above three strategic "resources" or competences, the ABO model fits well in today's dynamic milieu as its ethical approach along with all its rational and appropriate components aims at effective operation under able leadership with clear vision, incorporates the skill of team-building for required maturity, maintains its organisational culture and has a dynamic, decentralised and flexible organisational structure – moving towards encouraging innovations and "creative" personnel.

Such organisations will survive, grow and develop in the present business environment.

UTI Scam: Bereft of Trust

In 1999-2000, it was found that the Unit Trust of India (UTI) invested Rs 32 crore in a fake company whose share price was almost zero. UTI purchased the shares at the rate of Rs 10 per share. Since the company was declared to be in loss, UTI did not get any returns. Due to similar improper investments, the net asset value (NAV) of one unit of US-64 came down to less than Rs 10. Since the NAV was less than its face value, the scheme could not run smoothly. UTI had to stop trading of this scheme for six months, i.e., till January 2002. The chairman and two executive directors were remanded to CBI custody and had to finally resign.

The Zero Tolerance Model propounded by the former Chief Vigilance Commissioner, N. Vittal, is a commendable model to contain public corruption as in the case of UTI.

Zero Tolerance Model

Vittal propounded the following steps, among others, for containing public corruption through the Zero Tolerance Model. These steps are quite relevant to modern society.

Transparency International ranks countries on the basis of a corruption perception index. There is an urgent need to get a competent body like the IIMs, or industry associations academics or psephologists to list out in the order of the corruption perception index all government organisations, public sector enterprises and banks. The list must rank other organisations as well, such as all departments, ministries, public sector enterprises and banks, which are within the purview of the CVC. The need for such a listing is because of the recent World Bank observation that the Delhi Development Authority (DDA) is the most corrupt organisation in India. The World Bank report was based on the observations made by K.J. Alphons and this led to a protest by DDA officials. Last year, when someone observed that Delhi Air Customs was very corrupt, there was a strike which was ultimately called off after the striking employees had their way. A peculiar aspect of our government systems and public organisations is that while everybody will concede that these organisations are corrupt, the moment anyone makes a statement officially in a report or in public, it becomes a matter of defending the "fair name" of the office. As every office can harass the public and the rest of the government to by going on strike, they can have their way. This bluff must be called. In other words, zero tolerance of corruption should begin right here. The corruption perception index list must be published every year. We can then watch whether efforts are being made to bring down the level of corruption.

Intolerance of corruption can be bred in the culture of the people if we are able to use our education system to send the right signals. Like the National Cadet Corps, we should think of a National Vigilance Corps (NVC). We must encourage in colleges and educational institutions anti-corruption clubs which can work in close coordination with the CVC. The members of the NVC should be authorised to check and expose cases of corruption which will result ultimately in effective punishment. This may be one method by which the entire nation can be mobilised to fight corruption and the principle of zero tolerance will then have an added meaning.

E-governance and the Use of Information Technology to Check Corruption

This is the age of information technology (IT). The Prime Minister has gone on record to say that IT is India's tomorrow. In Andhra Pradesh we are seeing what is possible through the wide application of IT. The entire Government of India should move on to achieve e-governance. Using IT widely in all government departments will make it easy for every citizen who interacts with the government of India to get information freely and get his work done faster. For example, in Andhra Pradesh, the registration and transfer of property is done in a few hours instead of weeks or months as in other states. We can contrast the Andhra Pradesh experience with what happens in the DDA, where again we are dealing with transfer of property or the registration offices in Delhi and in other states. Extensive use of information technology to check corruption should be part of the zero tolerance approach to corruption.

Remove Obsolete Laws through Sunset Principles

Obsolete laws and time-consuming bureaucratic procedures are the breeding ground for corruption. We should implement throughout the Government of India the principle of sunset laws so that no law will be on the statute book for more than five or ten years unless it is re-enacted and re-promulgated after careful examination. This will automatically ensure that obsolete laws do not clutter the system.

The Government of India has already taken action to appoint the Jain Committee, which has recommended that out of the 2,500 administrative laws, about 1,300, should be scrapped. This can be done at one go so that the Government of India is not hampered by obsolete laws and time-consuming procedures, which are the breeding ground for corruption.

Implement the Benami Transactions (Prohibition) Act, 1988

Another action that can be taken immediately is to prescribe the procedure for confiscation of *benami* property under

Section 8 of the Benami Transaction Prohibition Act (BTPA). BTPA was passed in September 1988. It is surprising that even though Section 5 provides for the confiscation of *benami* property and Section 8 says that the government can prescribe rules for more than 11 years, nothing has been done by the government to prosecute the rules under this Act. In fact, the CVC took up the matter with the Revenue Department on January 7, 1999. The net result is that the Revenue Department now wants to scrap the Act. I can understand that if the Act is considered weak, it needs to be strengthened. The CVC must be empowered under this Act and not the income tax authorities. The chief technical examiner (CTE) of the CVC can be empowered to carry out the valuation process. The Law Commission fortunately does not think BTPA should be scrapped. The Supreme Court has upheld the validity of the Act and therefore it is high time rules were prescribed so that Benami property can be confiscated by the CVC so far as public servants are concerned.

Notes

1. Schuster, Frederick E., *Human Resource Management: Concepts, Cases and Readings*, Virgina, Reston Publishing Company, 1985, pp. 8-9.
2. Morita, Akio, *Made in Japan*, Collins, 1987 p.130.
3. Das Gupta, Ananda, *Anatomy of Human Resource Management: An Integrated Perspective, Management and Labour Studies*, XLRI, Jamshedpur, July 1996, pp. 147-157.
4. Das Gupta, Ananda, *Economic Programme for the Rural Poor: A Concept of Vivekananda in Swami Vivekananda and 21st Century,* Ed. Swami Someswarananda, Ramakrishna Mission, Khetri, 1993. pp. 79-82.
5. Swami Someswarananda: *Selecting the Right Candidate, Integral Management – Indian Perspective*, July-August 1991, pp. 2-4.

6. Khandwalla, P.N., *Organizational Designs for Excellence*, Tata McGraw Hill, New Delhi, 1992, pp. 218.
7. Hayes R.H. and Pisano, G.P., "Beyond World Class: The New Manufacturing Strategy", *Harvard Business Review*, January-February 1994 pp. 77-86.
8. C.K. & Hamel, G., "The Core Competence of the Corporation, *Harvard Business Review*, May-June 1990, pp. 79-91.

5

The Possible Way Out: Towards an Ethical Plateau?

The word "ethics" is defined as "the discipline dealing with what is good and bad and with normal duties and obligations". Thus, "personal ethics" have been referred to as "the rules by which an individual lives his or her personal life", and "accounting ethics" pertain to "the code that guides the professional conduct" of persons engaged in various activities. "Business ethics" are concerned with truth and justice and has a variety of aspects: market, society, corporate behaviour, et al. All three types of ethics are interrelated and each is the manifestation of the others.

Theories of Ethics

Three basic types of moral theories have been developed in the field of normative ethics. The First, the utilitarian theory, suggests that plans and actions should be evaluated by their consequences. The underlying idea is that plans or actions should produce the greatest good for the greatest number of people. The second theory is based on rights and holds that all people have basic rights, such as the right to freedom of conscience, free speech, due process and so on. The third

Figure 5.1

Decision Tree

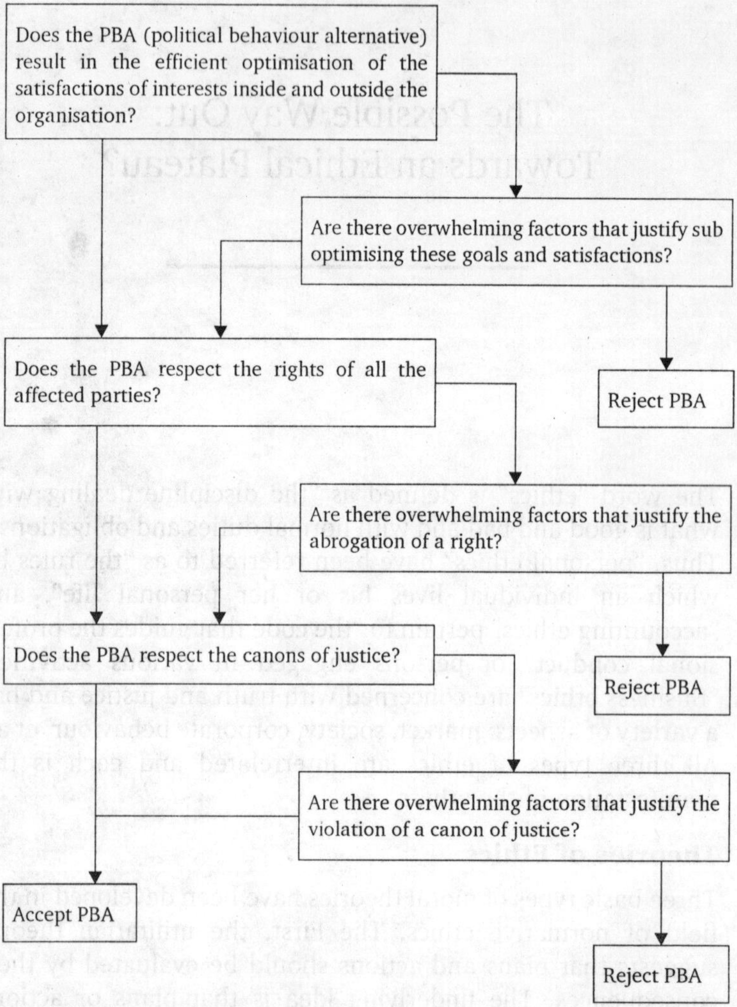

theory, the theory of justice, demands that decision-makers be guided by fairness and equity as well as impartiality. Cavanagh, Moberg and Valsquez[1] point out the strengths and weaknesses of each theory and integrate them into a decision tree (see Figure 5.1), which can guide decision-makers (bureaucrats/managers/politicians) in making ethical decisions.

Bernard[2] has described "moral behaviour" as behaviour "governed by beliefs or feelings of what is right or wrong regardless of self-interest or immediate consequences of a decision to do or not to do specific things under particular conditions".

Leys[3], on the other hand, illustrates the moral conflicts faced by decision-makers in a diagram (see Figure 5.2), in which moral standards surround action but, in which the standard at one arrow conflicts with the standard at the opposite arrow.

Figure 5.2

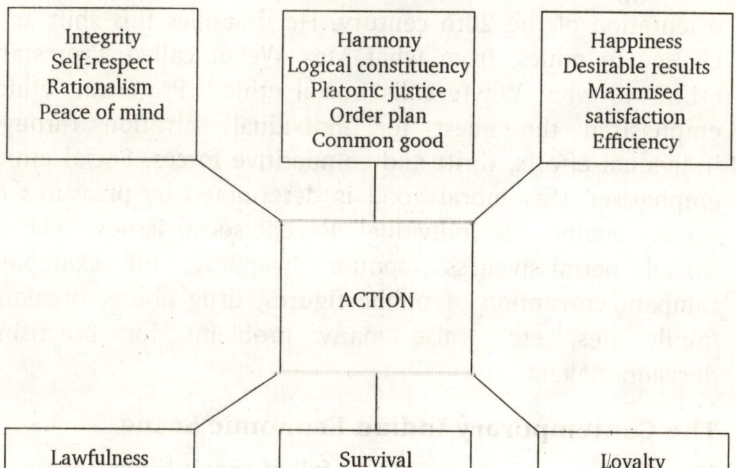

Reissman[4] describes changes in societies by distinguishing three types of men according to their source of moral direction: 1. the tradition directed type, 2. the inner directed type, and 3. other directed type.

The tradition directed type conforms to the culture and social order in which he lives. Society presents unchanging relationships that are accepted as right. Little effort is directed towards changing the status quo because it is considered wrong to break traditions. The inner directed man receives his source of direction early in life from his elders and develops a "psychological gyroscope" that keeps him on his moral course. The other directed man receives his sources of direction from his contemporaries and changes his concepts of what is right through a socialised sensitivity to the actions of others.

Closely related to Riesman's thinking, yet more pertinent to the decision maker's moral dilemma is the theory of William H. Whyte.[5] Whyte sees a major shift in western ideology from the rugged individualism of the 19th century to the social orientation of the 20th century. He describes this shift as a change in ethics, from what Max Weber called 'Protestant ethics' to what Whyte calls 'social ethics'. Protestant ethics emphasised the quest for individual salvation through individual efforts, thrift and competitive forces. Social ethics emphasised that moral good is determined by pressures of society against the individual. Recent social issues, such as sexual permissiveness (spouse swapping, for example), rampant corruption of public figures, drug abuse, breaking family ties, etc., raise many problems for practising decision-makers.

The Contemporary Indian Economic Scene

The Indian economic scenario is full of conundrums – bereft of ethics – full of squandering games by the politician-businessman-bureaucrat-landlord nexus, no accountability at any level, and commandos and terrorists ruling the roost. of public money have been spent on rural development programmes, yet no change is visible at the grassroots. They public sector is going the way of the dinosaur and the private sector is managing huge profits, sidewalking the importance of public disclosures. Ethics? No reply comes forth on this topic – either

Figure 5.3

Crises: Their Stages and Solutions

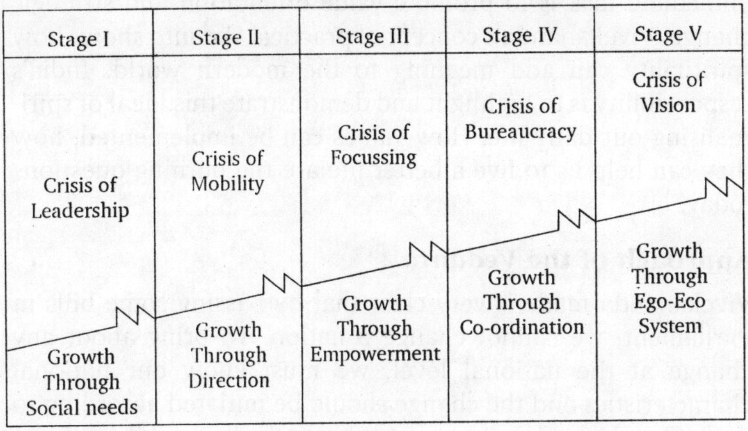

from the high-nosed professionals in their citadels of power or from the merchants, capitalists and landlords who have swarmed to the economic front of the country.

Let us now begin with some of the basic conundrums (Figure 5.3):

1. What is the present state? What is the extent of the crises?
2. In which direction should the change take place?
3. How can the desired change be brought about?
4. What should be the role of the change agent?
5. What should be its action plan?

The Present Indian State

What role has India to play in the world? Vivekananda clearly says that India's task is to make spirituality practical in every field. With the advancement of science and technology, people are giving more importance to the so-called objective world and material pleasures. They forget that life is a combination of subjective and objective elements. Unless we set a higher goal, materials goal will prove detrimental to human civilisation. This is what happened in ancient Rome.

Alvin Toffler has rightly said that "perpetual purposelessness" is the problem of the modern man. Thus, our immediate task is to promote value orientation and strategic change. Vivekananda's concept of practical *Vedanta* shows how spirituality can add meaning to the modern world. India's responsibility is to highlight and demonstrate this ideal of spiritualising our daily life. How values can be implemented, how they can help us to live a better life are the burning questions today.

Approach of the *Vedanta*

Vivekananda made it very clear that by passing some bills in Parliament, we cannot change a nation. To bring about any change at the national level, we must know our national characteristics and the change should be initiated according to those characteristics. So we must know the basic philosophy of the Indian mind. There are three basic points here:

1. Everybody has immense potential (*tat tvam asi*),
2. Holistic approach (*advaita* or the non-dual concept), and
3. Subjective elements are more powerful than objective elements (*sukshma* > *sthula*, or mind > matter).

These concepts of Indian origin are different from the western concepts. In the West, man is considered to be an elevated animal, while in India, man is the child of immortality (*amritasya putra*). Moreover, in the name of objectivity, the West lays more stress on matter and this has produced their material perspective.

Experiments Conducted by the Ramakrishna Mission

Though, according to western concepts, planning should be done at the top level and people should be involved in executing the plan, the Ramakrishna Mission (RKM) did just the opposite in more than 2,000 villages in West Bengal. RKM involved the people in identifying their problems, priorities, available resources, possible solutions, line of action and in executing and assessing their performance. Similar experiments were also carried out in villages in Maharashtra and Gujarat and in many public and private sector units where the workers could achieve their goals without any help from their superiors. These experiments show the validity of the principle given above, i.e., everybody has immense potential. And, in most of the cases, it was the mental block (subjective element), and not a resource crunch (objective element) that prevented them from throwing up ideas and solving their problems on their own.

Voluntary Organisations as Change Agents

Today, voluntary organisations can become an effective instrument in initiating a change for the purpose of initiating a people's movement to solve their problems. Therefore, let us examine the steps that voluntary organisations must take to bring about a change. These could be as follows:

1. Define the role of the organisation in society, i.e., its mission (social responsibility),
2. Set the goal (general and particular),
3. Point out the focus (the gap between the mission and the goal),
4. Suggest various possibilities to bridge the gap,
5. Draw up a treatment plan (strategic planning) through the participation of all the members, and
6. Implement change through the units of the organisation. Assess performance and re-adjust.

These are the basic tasks before any organisation. Once it is clear about its goal, the rest will be easier.

Today, our voluntary organisations can come up with bolder objectives. For example, Swami Someswarananda[6] suggests involving something like one lakh people in self-help community development projects like education, health, housing, self-employment, etc., in the next few months. If this can be implemented with a "bottom-up" approach, the people themselves can identify their problems, find available resources (both manpower and materials) in their locality, chalk out the action plan, execute it and assess their performance. The voluntary organisation's role would be just that of a catalyst, namely to inspire people and to help only when needed. The purpose, in Vivekananda's words, is to "open their eyes and give them back their lost identity and individuality".

Action Plan

The action by objective (ABO) theory exemplifies a method of self-control and the way of fixing a target with reference to one's own strengths and weaknesses to execute a project. It comprises the sequential conduct of the following four functions (Das Gupta, 1993):[7]

1. Reviewing and renovating strategies,
2. Providing a job improvement plan and congenial work environment,
3. Using present and potential performance reviews in a systematic way, and
4. Strengthening the ability and enriching the skills of the leaders through effective training and development.

In the ABO approach, the objectives are handed down with no spirit of authoritarianism and, as a tool for self-appraisal and self-development, it moves towards self-reliance, which has four components: (1) self-confidence, (2) better understanding, (3) team spirit, and (4) excellence in work, which again, in turn, as per the systems approach, will serve as "feedback elements" in a process of "taking from society" and "giving to society". The whole process increases the credibility of the review results and performance levels in the participatory approach under the "bottom-up" theory, under which "processing" in guided by ABO objectives.

Clarification of Some Doubts

But how will such projects, a sceptic may ask, help India to grow? The answer is:

The ultimate aim of the *Vedanta* is *moksha*. The way towards *moksha* is to become independent step by step. Such projects will help people move from dependence to interdependence. Today, people have become too dependent on the government. This attitude is, on one hand, making them helpless and, on the other, making the nexus more powerful. So, autonomy in the objective world is a great step towards independence and betterment.

Vedantic advaita (a holistic approach) will help people move from self-centredness to collective responsibility. It has been observed by many research groups that whenever a group of villagers or slum-dwellers are asked about their needs or problems, they immediately speak about their common problems. If people are involved in decision-making, they invariably take a holistic approach.

Vivekananda wanted to bring *shraddha* (faith) in the minds of the people. The projects and models described herein will help them inculcate self-respect; "sharing" will prevail over "grabbing".

Vivekananda spoke of a combination of democracy and socialism. He said that the enterprising character of democracy and the equality of socialism are to be blended. Many industries have implemented this *Vedanta* principle (Godrej on one extreme and Kamani on the other because Godrej implemented a philosophy and strategy of *kaizen*, which means changing the attitude of people towards improvements, and Kamani Tubes was taken over by the workers after it was declared "sick". The workers accepted the challenge of running the organisation successfully, and are now flourishing because they were both motivated and coordinated.

Ultimately, tasks of social transformation are not possible without the people gaining control over economic and social institutions, particularly in the context of unequal distribution of assets, both in the rural and urban areas. It will be necessary to build into economic programmes the conditions for facilitating the emergence and exercise of group power of the people at the grassroots level and also for influencing various policies at the national level.

Notes

1. Gerald F. Cavanagh, Dennis J. Meberg and Manuel Velasquez, "The Ethics of Organisation Politics", *Academy of Management Review*; July 1981, pp. 363-374. See also Moberg Cavanagh and Manuel Velasquez, "Organisational Politician", *Organisation Dynamics*, Autumn 1983, pp. 65-80.
2. Chester I. Bernard, "Elementary Conditions of Business Morals", *California Management Review*, Vol. 1. 1958, p.4.
3. Wayne A.R. Leys, "The Value Framework of Decision-Making", in *Concepts of Issues in Administrative Behaviour,* Eds. Sidney Mailick and Edward H. Van Ness, 1962.
4. David Riessman, *The Lonely Crowd*, Yale University Press, 1950.
5. William H. Whyte, *The Organisation Man*, New York, 1956.
6. Swami Someswarananda, "India Today", *Vedanta Kesari*, Chennai, September 1993.
7. Ananda Das Gupta, "Economic Programme for the Rural Poor: A Concept of Vivekananda", in *Swami Vivekananda and 21st Century,* Ramakrishna Mission, Khetri (Rajasthan), 1993.

6

Work Culture and Ethics

"We Indians suffer from a great defect, viz., we cannot make a permanent organisation and the reason is that we never like to share power with others and never think of what will come after we are gone."

—Swami Vivekananda

The human resource (HR) function has gradually shifted its focus from a narrow maintenance reactive role to a much wider canvas, integrating HR strategy with corporate strategy empowering employees, restructuring the organisation and so on (Monappa, 1997).[1]

Creative contributions (Hofstede, 1973)[2] in a globally cooperative situation would encompass the range of sub-systems from planning the numbers, types and skills of HR, ensuring their availability, placing in the right job, promoting and nurturing mental health and helping employees develop their special talents and skills.

In this process, new investments are needed to ignite a knowledge movement in the country. We must invest in training, re-training and continuous learning immediately, observes Ganguly,[3] otherwise, we will be left behind. This massive investment is focussed on re-profiting through on-job training, continuous learning of skills and having the competencies of managers and employees.

More recently, learning organisations (Senge, 1990)[4] and team-building concepts have emerged to serve as the basis for competitive advantage and for motivating employees in both the commitment and contribution necessary for organisational excellence in the fast-changing business scenario. Many large organisations are undertaking major restructuring to achieve a better "fit" and sensitivity to external demands (Genus, 1998).[5] A "new" model of organisation has emerged and knowledge about organisational design as a response to environmental challenges has got further refined in the 1990s. Some of the key features of this new model of organisations are that they are networked, flat, flexible and global. Figure 6.1 below summarises the shift which has occurred in organisations and which has led to the emergence of HRM in response to the demands and exigencies of the new organisation:

Figure 6.1

Old Model	**New Model**
Individual position/ job as basic unit of organisation	Team as a basic unit
Relations with environment handled by specialists	Densely networked with environment
Vertical flows of information	Horizontal and vertical flows of information
Tall (many layers of management)	Flat (few layers of management)
Emphasis on structures	Emphasis on process
Career paths upwards/linear	Career paths flexible/lateral
Standardised evaluation and reward systems	Customised evaluation and reward systems.
Ethnocentric	International
Single strong culture with strong expectations of behaviour	Diversity of viewpoints and behaviour

Source: Adapted from Ancona et al., "The "New" Organization", 1996.

Conventional personnel management appears to be a part of an old model of organisation or of a more mechanistic organisation, which is more bureaucratic in nature having lesser flexibility, higher amount of centralisation and a higher formalisation level, i.e., adherence to rules and regulations.

Human resource management (HRM), on the other hand, is compatible with the new model of organisation and has emerged to align with the organic design of organisations which have cross-functional and cross-hierarchical teams, and are decentralised and flexible with a low formalisation level and a wider span of control.

Interestingly, Guest[6] has drawn a beautiful line between personnel management and HRM (Figure 6.2).

Figure 6.2

Stereotypes of Personnel Management and HRM

Dimensions	Personnel Management	HRM
Time and planning perspective	Short-term, ad hoc	Long-term, pro-active
Psychological contract	Compliance	Commitment
Control systems	External control	Self-control
Employee relations perspective	Pluralist, collective low-trust	Individual developed
Preferred structures/systems	Bureaucratic	Organic developed
Roles	Formal, defined roles	Flexible roles
Evaluation criteria	Cost minimisation	Maximum utilisation (human asset accounting)

With all these new changes taking place in the realm of HR, we need to develop a "strong" work culture within the organisation to provide a wider base for holistic development.

Based on the principles of management theory, the four factors are identified here to develop work culture in an organisation:

Vision

Vision is not merely a long-term objective, but a company's perspective. It indicates the legacy it would like to pass on to its succeeding generation of leaders; it is a statement which inspires its employees with a dream, goal and generates pride in them. The key question the organisation should ask itself is: What do we want to be known for?

Basically, this has two key dimensions:

1. To try and prove that an organisation, when deeply committed to its values, is best equipped to lead society to a better life, and
2. To strengthen the organisation's base through the effective utilisation of men and materials.

Mission

While a vision denotes a broad general picture, a mission hones it to focus and concentrates on a particular area.

Values

According to ethical concepts applied in management, values indicate the relationship one has with others. The suggestion in the Upanishads, *Saha nau bhunaktu* (let us all share together), implies cooperation, harmonisation, combined benefits for oneself, collaborators and society, trust and a pro-active desire for others' success.

Strategy

There are two aspects of strategy: internal and external. Internal strategy should involve employees by generating a feeling of ownership and belongingness towards the organisation, which naturally generates quality and excellence. Along with this, innovation and growth are also essential factors and must be sustained by focussing on the *sukshma* aspect (micro aspect). Continuous growth can be achieved by each unit and person trying to beat their previous performance. Growth does not only mean profit and turnover, but mainly a transformation (Someswarananda, 1996).[7]

Now obviously, the question arises of how to implement the four key factors of vision, mission, values and strategy, which are conducive to the enhancement of work culture development in an organisation?

The techniques which are basically holistic in nature, have a SEWA (self-mastery, empathy for workers, worker directedness and achievement in performance) approach in their application. This approach is called action by objective (ABO) (Das Gupta, 1995)[8] and is discussed here to provide a broad-based understanding of an "enlightened" organisation which has developed a work-culture within its milieu fully well.

As Vivekananda (1992: 46) put it: "Karmayoga is the attaining through unselfish work of that freedom which is the goal of all human nature ...... Karmayoga, therefore, is a system of ethics and religion intended to attain freedom through unselfishness, and by good works".[9] The ABO model consciously underlines the importance of freedom and that is why the approach is free from any sort of "tyranny". The automotive mechanism for self-appraisal, and thereby scope for self-development, has been focussed in this model which, in turn, leads a team towards self-reliance when it attains self-confidence (quoting Vivekananda: "The old religion said that he was an atheist who did not believe in God. The new religion says that he is the atheist who does not believe in himself") and is armed with better understanding to combat the environment – both internal and external (developing power capabilities for dealing with environment), reinforced by a team-spirit, which finally results in excellence in work. The ABO model starts with, as we observe, four basic components. As a team, through sharing and the process of harmonisation, all review and renovate strategies, according to both the short-term and long-term needs and objectives/goals of the organisation. This method helps them prepare a job improvement plan in a congenial work environment. On attaining the short-and medium-term objectives, there should be an opportunity for the team to review its performance in a systematic way so that it can forge ahead by strengthening, its abilities and enriching its skills. The team which we are referring to consists of both managers and shop-floor workers along with mid-level supervisors, thus providing a holistic idea about a team which can visualise, take up missions, fix up strategies and utilise values as essential tools.

But how will such projects, a sceptic may ask, help organisations to grow? The answer is:

Two empirical evidences (Kalburgi, 1995)[10] of the ABO spirit can be put forward here to highlight the principles enshrined therein:

Yash Paper Mills in Uttar Pradesh has a unionised workforce of about 200. A collective bargaining contract governs employee compensation and other due processes. The company has been reorganised along Indian ethos notions. The nine departments have been given Hindi names such as Jankari Sevak Sangh, Kagaz Vyapar Sangh, Kachha Maal Vyapar Sangh, etc. Each sangh is headed by a Samrakshak. Each Sangh elects a Pradhan for a one-year period who in turn selects a Sahayak from within the Sangh. Each Sangh holds a weekly meeting chaired by the Samrakshak or Pradhan or Sahayak and reviews the outputs and problems encountered in the previous week and tries to anticipate and prevent or counter problems in the coming week. Decisions are consensus based. Decisions that involve other Sanghs are made at the weekly meetings of the Samrakshaks, again on a consensus basis. There is a monthly bonus linked to production and productivity. The absolute amount of bonus is the same for everybody in the company, even though the salaries are different and based on job classification. The company is getting 120 per cent commitment from its employees. The employees feel it is their company, that it is their extended family.

Adaipur in Gujarat is a small village of about 600 families. It used to be riddled with factions that indulged in political infights. A few years ago, the villagers became Swadhyayees one by one. And today almost all belong to the Swadhyaya movement. Swadhyaya means self-learning or self-developm-ent and discovery of one's own identity in a spiritual sense, a process of realisation that the individual self is indeed the same as the Supreme Self (*Aham Brahmasmi*).

Covey[11] spoke about principle-centred leadership which is nothing but leadership centring on fairness, kindness, efficiency and effectiveness. It also includes genuineness of purpose and transparency in execution. The emerging international economic architecture is bringing about a competitive world with a solid work culture base to face challenges with courage, conviction and innovativeness.

Notes

1. Arun Monappa, *Managing Human Resource*, New Delhi, 1997.
2. H.G. Hofstede, "Frustrations of Personnel Managers", *Management International Review*, Vol. 13, 1973.
3. Ashok Ganguly, "The Road Ahead", *Excellence in the 21st Century: Challenges and Strategies*, AIMA, New Delhi, 1998.
4. Peter Senge, *The Fifth Discipline: The Art & Practice of The Learning Organization*, England, 1990.
5. Audley Genus, *The Management of Change: Perspective and Practices*, London, 1998.
6. D. Guest, "Human Resource Management and Industrial Relations," *Journal of Management Studies*, 24 (5), 1987.
7. Swami Someswarananda, *Indian Wisdom for Management*, AMA, Ahmedabad, 1996.
8. Ananda Das Gupta, "Economic Management and Ethics: The Vedantic Answer", *Indian Journal of Public Administration*, New Delhi, July-September 1995.
9. *Perennial Vivekananda: A Selection*, Sahitya Akademi, New Delhi, 1992.
10. Kalburgi Srinivas, "Indian Ethos in Management: A Subjective Prognosis", *Abhigyan*, New Delhi, Spring, 1995.
11. Stephen R. Covey, *Principle-Centred Leadership*, London, 1992.

7

Corporate Ethics: Dilemmas, Constraints and Pace Settings

We can still recollect the comments made by Warren Anderson, chairman of Union Carbide, soon after the Bhopal gas tragedy of December 1984, in which 6,000 people perished and 2,00,000 others were injured. He said he would spend the rest of his life attempting to correct the sufferings his company had caused and trying to make amends One year later, he reversed his earlier "emotional reaction", saying that he had "overreacted" and was now prepared to lead the company in its legal battle against paying damages and representations. As has been observed elsewhere (Mander, 1996),[1] Anderson first reacted as a human being and then as the chairperson of Trans National Company (TNC) whose obligations are to the hundreds of thousands rich shareholders from the global north.

This unethical culture is part of the tenets of free market capitalism, which has spread its tentacles all over the world in search of cheap extraction and labour, lucrative markets and eternal financial .growth. This new economics in search of never-ending growth is far removed from the ethical concerns expressed throughout history by key economic thinkers from Adam Smith to Karl Marx and John Maynard Keynes. An economics devoid of equity, ecology and ethics is a most dangerous academic myth. For both Adam Smith and Marx, the foundation of economic thinking was based on more fundamental ethical questions and deep-rooted humanism.

This ethical underpinning of economics is what is lacking in the increasingly mechanical and mathematical theorisation of monetarism and neo-liberal theories of "growth" measured in terms of GDP and "competitiveness" but never in terms of the ecological and social costs of that "growth". The bandwagon of sustainable "economic growth" is based on the myth that there can be eternal growth if we leave everything in the "invisible" hands of the market. However, such an assumption fails to acknowledge the fact that the economy is an "open subsystem, which is finite, non-growing and materially closed". Unless we consider the depletion of natural resources, the cost of pollution, human rights violation, informal work in households, particularly by women, social tension and a growing sense of physical and emotional insecurity, the present parameters of economic growth can be dangerously misleading. An economic paradigm that talks about accumulation and consumption signifies the greed of the few rather than the need of everyone.

In any engagement or dialogue with corporations, it is important to remember that corporations are very clear about their agenda: they are very clear about how they want to go about their trade as well as their public policy agenda. This is not the case with activist groups, consumer organisations and human rights groups. They are not clear about what they want and how they should achieve it. This is because of the multiple perspectives and interests that inform the action groups. As a result, corporations often co-opt language, people and programmes to give the impression that they care. Most of them don't. That is what happened with the campaign against the Enron power projects near Mumbai. In the beginning, Enron adopted a confrontationist approach with local activist groups, but when they found themselves cornered, they changed their strategy. They coopted not only language, but also erstwhile activists with good job offers and local NGOs with funds. The language, style and format of Enron's public relations magazine resembled that of NGOs. They called it *Dialogue* and one of the first issues had a screaming headline: "Struggle Ends and Dialogue Begins". Enron widely publicised its 'income generation' activities by distributing a few sewing machines to women and its ecological sensitivity by planting a few saplings. By changing their strategy, by using buzzwords such as "community empowerment" and "ecological sensitivity", the company actually changed the rules of the game in their favour without changing their flawed basic philosophy and operational strategies.

The experiment of ACCORD in the Nilgiri in South India and the formation of a successful cooperative movement by tribals to plant, pluck, pack, brand and market tea is an inspiring example of a viable alternative. The Adivasi Munneta Sanghatana (trade union of tribal farmers and workers) promoted by ACCORD over a period of ten years not only managed to form and run the tea cooperatives but also succeeded in market intervention by changing the rules of pricing. In collaboration with the Students Solidarity group, the tea cooperative purchased its own plantation and thereby, a substantial increase in their bargaining power.

The initiative of Navsarjan, a Dalit action group in Gujarat, to introduce social security packages to thousands of its members through a people-friendly insurance scheme, is another laudable alternative effort. The chain of Indian Coffee Houses in different parts of India is also, run using cooperative ethics.

The Kutch Mahila Vikas Sangh and SEWA in Gujarat have proved the market potential of such endeavours. All over the world, there are many such new initiatives and experiments. However, the force of the big corporations and their advertising war is so severe that these small initiatives become invisible in the brand-marketing blitz. Hence, there is a need to document such innovative experiences and alternatives and to build mutually enabling relationships between them.

When we think of corporate angles, we live in a time when cataclysmic revolutions and promising egalitarian utopias have been discredited. But, the urge to ensure a basic livelihood for all remains strong and it is not committed to passionately dedicated social activists on the fringes of society. It is obvious to some people in the mainstream of economic activity that the long-term sustainability of their business depends on the health of the environment and society at large. And, thus, it is unacceptable that millions of people continue to live in an economic and ecological wasteland. For then, "order" would, eventually, have to be enforced by armed militias.

Therefore, many large corporations are finding sound business sense in being more socially accountable. This is quite different from corporate philanthropy, which means giving large donations to community projects, the arts and humanitarian charities. Corporate social responsibility is about modifying, or even re-making, the ethical basis on which corporations conduct their business. At the same time, most such corporations are also fostering a form of globalisation that threatens to drive millions of people deeper into poverty. Is there a silver lining to this paradox?

The Current American Scenario

Time appears to be running out for those who are content to maximise profits with minimal regard for the social, economic and environmental impact of their business. More and more American and European investors are looking for stocks in which they can invest with a clear conscience. For example, a little while ago, the American biotechnology multinational company, Monsanto, saw its share price nosedive due to public protests about its genetically modified products.

Even Wall Street has responded to this trend, with the Dow Jones launching a sustainability group index (SGI) sometime ago. This listing automatically excludes companies involved in gambling or alcohol manufacturing. The SGI rates companies for their success in managing economic, environmental and social factors. Of the top 2,000 companies listed with the Dow Jones, only about 200 qualified for selection on the new index. The San Francisco-based group, Business for Social Responsibility, has been working since 1992 to help companies sustain their commercial success "in ways that demonstrate respect for ethical values, people, communities and the environment". This group already has 1,400 member companies and their affiliates, which employ a total of six million workers. Among the member companies are American Express, AT&T Dupont, Ford, General Motors, Johnson and Johnson and Levi Strauss.

Now, let us see what are the kind of changes that would bring about true liberalisation. That would mean giving a real chance to the enterprising energies and creativity of people on the lowest rungs of the socio-economic ladder. This question is not yet at the forefront of the debate on corporate social responsibility in the West. And it's certainly not in India.

Yet, the possibility of injecting this dimension could be waiting in the wings. Interestingly, one of the most indicting reports on India's environmental and livelihood crisis has come from a corporate sector body, the Tata Energy Research Institute. The study, sponsored by 11 of India's biggest companies, was published in 1998 and was titled "Looking Back to Enhancement of Environment and Nature". The document paints a grim picture of ecological degradation across the sub-continent and also places a monetary value on this damage. For example, the "annual economic value" of the impact of the poor quality of drinking water has been estimated at Rs 122 billion. The adverse effects on human health due to polluted air are estimated at over Rs 855 billion.

The idea that environmental and social equity concerns somehow hold back progress and growth is still around. True liberalisation would involve policies and business practices, which see the hidden opportunities in this crisis. And, these must be opportunities for every last Indian, not merely the top 25 per cent of the population. Currently, the reverse is true. A wide variety of alternative perspectives on modes of production and building of infrastructure are still knocking on the gates of corporate India.

Another promise of the possibilities is faintly visible in the glare of adulation that follows the two icons of India's corporate sector, namely, Azim Premji of Wipro and N.R. Narayana Murthy of Infosys. It is neither accidental not incidental that both these chief executives are frequently talking about their commitment to the value of trusteeship. Fulfilling the promise of this commitment is not only their individual responsibility, it is a collective institutional exercise that needs a wide range of passionate energies. The Tata code of conduct, on the other hand, summarises the following things:

The Tata Code of Conduct

In 1998, the Tatas adopted a code of conduct, which covers both the operations of its companies and employees.

The code enjoins the companies which sign it to, among other things:

1. Supply goods and services of the highest quality standards to ensure the total satisfaction of customers.
2. Engage only in activities beneficial to the national interest of the country they operate in.
3. Be fully transparent in accounting and financial reporting standards.
4. Fully strive for the establishment and support of a competitive open market economy and to abhor unfair trade practices.
5. Be equal opportunity employers.
6. Neither give nor take any illegal payment, remuneration, gift, donation or comparable benefit to obtain business or favours.
7. Not give any donation to any government agency or its representatives to obtain any favourable performance of official duties.
8. Not support any specific political party or candidate for political office.

9. Comply with all regulations regarding the preservation of the environment.
10. Be a good corporate citizen, and to actively assist in the improvement of the quality of life of the community with the objective of making it self-reliant. These social activities are regarded as an integral part of their business plans and not as an optional part.
11. Cooperate and share physical, human and management resources with other Tata companies so along as this does not adversely affect its business interests and shareholder value.

In an article, 'New Age for Business', which appeared in *Fortune* magazine (1990), Frank Rose reports and comments on a new framework that is emerging for viewing and understanding business – a new paradigm that will carry humankind beyond the industrial age to the mental and spiritual enrichment of those who take part in it. The article highlights the following: "Visionary thinkers are rejecting the by-the-numbers approach to enterprise and seeking a new paradigm for viewing the world. Love and caring in the workplace? The profit motive less than pre-eminent? Major corporations are buying in."

The Alacrity Foundation was launched in 1978 by Amol Karnard and this consists of Alacrity Foundations (P) Ltd., Alacrity Housing Ltd., and Alacrity Electronics Ltd., largely as an expression of search for an integrated identity in a complex society through the medium of business. Some friends and family members of Karnard joined the new venture.

The active practice of ethical leadership meant that the promoters had to remove the dividing line between personal life and professional life and be open, predictable and accountable with one another first and then behave similarly with constituents outside Alacrity. The promoters decided that this need would be best served if they not only worked together, but also lived together, which promoted Alacrity's first apartment construction. Today, the Alacrity brand carries as much value in government departments as elsewhere in the marketplace.

There are some observations made which are pertinent to our topic of discussion, i.e., corporate ethics:

1. The Alacrity group's current annual turnover is in the region of Rs 100 crore.
2. Alacrity Housing Ltd. is an overwhelming market leader among flat builders in the city of Chennai. It has paid steady dividends to its shareholders from the first full year of its operations.
3. Alacrity Electronics Ltd., which has a significant presence in the field of energy management with the well-established Krykard brand, opened its dividend records in 1999.
4. Alacrity Foundations Pvt. Ltd. has emerging business in the fields of primary healthcare and education.
5. Even more striking has been its social performance.
   (a) Alacrity is in a position to say today that more than 30 percent of the flat building activity in Chennai is in strict accordance with development control regulations and free from black money.
   (b) Nearly 30 per cent of Alacrity's labour force has shown itself capable of sustained employment and earnings, thereby opening the prospect of an extended market for housing and growing opportunities for employment to cover the less privileged in our society.
   (c) Alacrity's top managers mostly stay in Alacrity flats, travel by two-wheelers or public transport and draw salaries much less than what they would command elsewhere in the market. In the process, they demonstrate that a moderate lifestyle does not stand in the way of excellence in business performance.

At the end, we might as well ask, "Are we not making it all sound a little too smooth and rosy? Problems and crises were there. To meet such demanding standards over long years, Alacrity's managers have had to sustain a level of self-discipline, commitment and self-renewal that can, at times, become quite stressful, especially at the higher levels. This would perhaps explain a recent development, which tested the institution's strength: A group of senior employees departed from the Alacrity fold, but the company came through this test quite well. There is enough evidence to show that the institution has only grown wiser and stronger after every fresh crisis. And it continues to have the conviction that no wealth or power can be more valuable than its dignity, no loss of profit can be more critical than the loss of its credibility, no skill or qualifications can substitute for the integrity of its character. As a result, the dangers and risks are turned into opportunities and the failures become the proverbial stepping stones to success.

No Dirty Tactics: Compaq Computers

Zarir Batliwala, director of human resources and company secretary of Compaq Computers in India, in an interview, revealed that his company has followed core values and a code of conduct for all members of the organisation.[2] It covers the expanse from financial irregularities to sexual harassment. Ethics is actively implemented in the organisation. All new trainees are handed a copy. At training sessions, they are asked to talk about the ethical code. Every year, an EHS (environment health and safety) audit is conducted. According to Batliwala, a written ethical code reinforces what we already know. It is really good for somebody who has never really thought about these issues. But the absence of a written code encourages immoral behaviour. One can still follow one's conscience.

He further admitted that it would be hypocrisy to pretend that profit is not the main motivator. But any forward-looking ethical company will agree that it has an obligation to the community as well. There should be a policy, for this, which may not be all-encompassing. That would be unrealistic. But there should be commitment in terms of resource management and recycling. There will always he companies which don't care. But as they match global standards of disclosure, there will be more and more ethical treatment of the environment.

The Way Out: Corporate Citizenship

According to the *Vedanta*, everybody is potentially divine; according to Christianity and Islam, God created men and women. And God's creation cannot be unholy. As all religions speak of the inherent divinity of men and women, there should not be any discrimination based on sex, caste, religion, language, etc. This equality should be a must for all.

As a person is, social being, he cannot live in isolation, he is a part of society. Similarly, every community is a part of society, and to grow, each community must live in harmony, every community has to help others. Society must be looked at in its totality, instead of taking a one-dimensional approach. Vivekananda says that the downfall of Indians started when they created the word, *mleccha* (outcaste, foreigner).

All religions are essentially the same. They all say that one has to cultivate truthfulness, honesty, caring for others, etc., if one wants to be religious. And regarding the goal, one religion asks us to be God, another tells us to realise God, still another directs us to go to God. Now what does God mean? It means "perfection". So all the religions ask us to be perfect.

Diversity is the sign of life, Swamiji points out; and at the same time, he asks us to notice the unity also. There is nothing wrong in following one's own way of spiritual practice, but one should notice the underlying unity of all religions. This is the democratic approach. Our future lies in harmonising there two.

The present world-view is based on two fundamentally wrong principles and our thinking needs to shift from a world-view based on:

1. Separateness to unity (concept of *Advaita*, i.e., oneness), and
2. Objective focus of attention to subjective focus of attention (mind is more powerful than matter).

The present age focusses its attention on the objective. It deals with everything on the basis of its objective reality. The other view is that it is the subjective that should be the focus of attention. Obviously if you focus on the subjective, then it automatically takes care of the objective also. Thus, a focus on the subjective is more holistic. However, if we concentrate all the time on the objective reality, then we tend to forget the subjective and this is what we have done today.

The present thinking or our sickness is based on a fundamental error. This may be called the error of separation.

We separate mind from matter, man from others, one man from another man, life from work, observer from the observed, sin from religion, gains from long term harm, etc.

In today's view, atomic particles are taken as objective reality. Thus, in the last three-four centuries, the whole has been based on this separateness and our entire world-view is based on this separateness.

There is another view which is not of separateness, but of "oneness" or "unity". When we talk about this unity, we are also aware of this feeling of separateness, but it only means a clear understanding of the limits of separateness and also realising at the same time that at one level, there is unity. Therefore, we only restrict the domain of separateness and recognise the domain of unity. The moment we understand this concept of unity of existence and interconnectedness, there is a tremendous change in our world-view. We see the logical necessity to bring back a sense of values in all that we do.

Therefore, the new paradigm in management is to recognise this unity and the importance of the subjective focus of attention, which is the cause of the objective reality. This is the essential shift in management. Applying the *Vedanta* principle has shown how it will help people in every sphere of life. The *Vedanta* can answer the crucial questions the modern world is facing; its science, sociology and philosophy will find its culmination in the *Vedanta*. If we are to grow, if we are to survive in the 21st century, we have to bring the *Vedanta* into management concepts and practices.

This feeling of oneness leads to a new way of handling of organisations. It discourages one to control from the top. It leads one to participative work, a feeling of responsibility at all levels. This unity leads to empowering people rather than authoritatively controlling them. It leads to a sense of participative culture in which every individual in the organisation shares the responsibility of achieving the goal, depending upon the sphere of his expertise and skill. Finally, it brings the attention of the individuals from the objective reality of things to the subjective reality. It means a process of going inwards to understand the outward things.

The urgent challenge before us is one of improving competitiveness, which means that we must have the latest technology, our products must meet international standards of quality, we must keep costs under control and we must be totally committed to customer service and satisfaction. We have to make our motto: Excellence in work is yoga.

The new environment will open up fresh opportunities and challenges not only to the present generation, but to how we take care of the future generations. We must realise that any waste of inefficiency in any sector of the economy ultimately impinges on the cost of goods and services produced anywhere in the country. Resource exploitation and depletion of natural resources, deforestation, pollution, etc. pose a threat to the environment itself.

Moreover, the general masses are hoping for deliverance from the misery of poverty and economic backwardness. The mass media has generated aspirations and expectations, especially in the rural interiors, and made them more aware of and demanding about their role in society, whether as consumers, employees, investors, business associates or ordinary citizens.

In the name of caring for people, public sector companies concentrate only on the employees and not customers. Because of strong union activities, employees have taken it for granted that their job is eternally secure. As a result, product quality caring for customers is neglected. Too many checks and controls and time-bound promotions have dampened the spirit. The main problem here is lack of motivation. Further, as very few are willing to take responsibility and make quick decisions to solve customer problems, red-tapism and status quo prevail.

On the other hand, in many private sector companies, money-spinning attitudes and corrupt practices in the name of competition run the show.

Swami Vivekananda has made it clear that "*atmano-mokshartham jagat-hitay ca*" (coordination of private and public benefit) is the best policy. An employee cannot survive if he does not help his company to grow, and a company cannot grow at the cost of the society.

The real issue then becomes to drive people's action towards the ultimate purpose of life – joy. Service which is rendered without any joy helps neither the server nor the served. But all other pleasures and possessions pale into nothingness before service which is rendered in a spirit of joy. This basic truth of life has to be reinstated in the minds of the people. They have forgotten this and are moving towards disaster.

While many modern management tools from the West as well as Japan have been found useful, it is now increasingly recognised that our own social values have a predominant influence in successfully managing industrial enterprises in our country. This raises the issue of attitudes of employees and the changing role of managers in the day-to-day running of businesses. No social, national or organisational perfection is possible without individual perfection. Hence, there is a need for inspiring and motivating managers to adapt for themselves a deliberate plan of self-development.

We forget that it is the cause that produces the effect, that the effect cannot come by itself; unless the cause is proper and powerful, the effect will not be produced. Today, the tendency to earn "quick money" has eaten away the national fabric.

Caring for customers and quality products are the most important factors in industry and business. Solving problems of the people/society should be a corporate mission.

1. Data may be objective, but a decision is subjective in most cases. You can draw different conclusions from the same set of data. Now this data or fact gets distorted by a narrow mind, whether in politics or in industry; many leaders have lost their credibility because of their partisan approach. The mind should not be biased, it should be impartial.
2. On attitude towards work, the secret, Vivekananda says, is to put our whole minds into our work, but not to get attached. We have to reserve the power of detaching ourselves from everything, however beloved, however much the soul might yearn for it, however great the pangs of misery we feel on leaving it, and still reserve the power of leaving it whenever we want.
3. "Work, Ask nothing in return. Give what you have to give. It will come back multiplied a thousandfold, but the attention must not be on that. Learn that the whole of life is giving, that nature will force to give."

The basic principle of Indian wisdom is: "Each soul is potentially divine"; "*Aham Brahmasmi*": I can make the impossible possible; "*Tattvamasi*": Everybody can make himself a genius. Swamiji says asserting one's spiritual nature makes one stronger.

As Swami Vivekananda puts it: *Atmano-mokshartham-jagat-hitaya ca*-from our own salvation (upliftment) and for the good of the world. Synchronise your private benefit with the public benefit, the ultimate goal being happiness and harmony.

What is work? Karma is to be done in the spirit of *yajna* (helping each other), instead of competition (an I-win-you-lose policy). This principle helps to bring about harmony in society. This leads us to the question of having an appropriate organisation culture, keeping the principle of *yajna* in mind.

How to work? Through *seva* and *tyaga*. *Seva* means to serve others and *tyaga* means to give one's best for the good of others. The health of a company depends upon "how best it can satisfy the needs of its customers", and profit will automatically follow. Swami Vivekananda, time and again, highlighted the concepts of *seva* and *tyaga*.

Spirit of work: *Yoga karmashu kaushalam* (excellence in work is yoga). Excellence is a continuous process. While playing a complementary role to others, compete with yourself – make your performance better than the previous one. Try to give your best, show your excellence. The attitude of excellence with the spirit of *seva* helps one to gain credibility in the market. If you specialise in a product or raw material or technology, the future is uncertain as there is constant change in these three. So, specialise in the problems of people and solve these with the help of your product or service.

Inner resources (courage, vision, insight, etc.) are more powerful than external resources (land, capital, etc.). The *Vedanta* says, *sukshma* (subtle, subjective) factors are more powerful and important than the *sthula* (gross, objective) once.

Most of the problems are subjective. About 80 per cent of management is man management. Data may be objective, but decisions are subjective. Thus, decision-making based on this principle along with the other principles of *karma yoga* though *yajna-seva-tyaga* offers a better solution.

Indian philosophy has shown that one never finds peace in maximising of consumption. Restraint is the key word. The West has been saying that restraint on consumption will restrict progress and affect the growth rate. This excessive emphasis on consumption preached by the West has brought us to a point of zero or negative growth because all our resources are being depleted. Indian wisdom has rightly pointed out the difference between a "high standard of life" and "high standard of consumption".

Happiness (*ananda*, the ultimate goal, arises out of practice of *dharma*, i.e., values of life, following the principles of good conduct, like unselfish performance of duties with love, respect for others, dedication, etc.

* * *

In man-centred philosophy, every cognitive enterprise is value-oriented. In the Indian tradition, the activity of man, reflective of his cognition, desire, deliberation and choice comprises, four *purusartha* (values): *dharma* (moral value, duty), *artha* (economic value), *kama* (hedonistic value) and *moksha* (spiritual value).

As a human value, *purusartha* is to be achieved by conscious efforts at self-cultivation the individual. *Purusartha* is the satisfaction of human desire. We live at two levels – organic and hyper-organic. *Kama* and *artha* – physical and economic values – belong to the organic level. Values of association and fellowship, the intellectual, moral aesthetic and religious values, belong to the hyper-organic level. All such higher values of life are included in *dharma* and *moksha*.

But again, apart from the rhetoric, reality haunts us by way of subjecting man to a rigorously mechanised, corporate way of living where he is reduced merely to a machine, which ultimately leads to "estrangement". Estrangement refers to what can be called "work estrangement" – gradual slackening of dedication towards eagerly chosen tasks (Lal, 1997).[3] In order to overcome estrangement, Lal (ibid.) suggests that man take the cue from Shankya, *manana*.

"...*manana* is the (only) way to meet every kind of estrangement. Such a persistent indulgence in thinking will keep one conscious of himself, and the moment this element of I-awareness is introduced in life's scheme, the process of the conquest of estrangement comes to life" (ibid.). The value orientations of Indian philosophy increase man's knowledge and his competence for performance. They also endow him with the power of discrimination and judgement.

Millennium Lessons for New Generation Managers

The *Gita* speaks of three different ways of reaching one's goal: *jnana yoga* (through knowledge), *karma yoga* (through dutybound activities) and *bhakti yoga* (through devotion to work). Each of these is capable of taking the individual to perfection. Man can go beyond the fetters of his body and it is the realisation of him as a pure being in and through all the levels of his existence (here we may recall the Habermasean concept for relevance and beyond) which seems to be the motto of good corporate citizenship. This realisation is realisation of freedom itself, which is blissful in its nature.

According to Aurobindo, the true conception of the Ultimate Reality should be such that it is both theoretically consistent and practically realisable. He has put emphasis on the self-preparation that is absolutely necessary for expediting the process of evolution from the mind to the super mind. For this he has advocated integral *yoga* (*purna* yoga) which is a harmony of wisdom, love and affection.

Integral *yoga* has the following objectives in view:

1. It aims at total transformation,
2. It aims at dynamic union with being (the self and the ultimate), and
3. It aims at the collective liberation of mankind.

According to this theory, personal liberation cannot be the highest end of life. When mankind is liberated collectively, there will be a unique world order ruled by spiritual values.

Cases from Japan: Morality at Stake?

Cases of Japanese corporations violating business ethics show up in the news one after another. To name but a few, there are the payoffs to *sokaiya* (corporate racketeers) by Ajinomoto, Takashimaya, and Nomura Securities; huge loans to *sokaiya* without adequate collateral by Daiichi Kangyo Bank; and the disclosure of unfair trade in copper by Sumitomo Corporation.

Unity of Morality and Economy

Shibusawa Eiichi (1841-1931), an important businessman and business leader at the dawn of capitalism in Japan, during the

Meiji period (1868-1912), called for the "unity of morality and the economy", urging businessmen to hold "the *Analects of Confucius* in one hand, an abacus in the other". Although allowing that businessmen must earn money, Shibusawa cautioned against the use of unethical practices to do so.

Shibusawa said: "(A business that) founders by holding to morals is not a failure. (A business that) prospers without holding to morals is not a success."

He also said: "(He who) seeks fame and fortune through immorality, misconduct and deception will never achieve it. Even if he achieves temporary fame and fortune through some stroke of luck, it will be only as a floating cloud in the heavens, soon to be dispersed by a gust of wind."

Shibusawa's words apply just as well to today's world of business management. Author Shiroyama Saburo, who deeply sympathises with Shibusawa's life philosophy, titled his biographical novel about the man, *Brave and Fearless*.

Shibusawa worked to foster and strengthen industry through the establishment of the Daiichi National Bank and Oji Paper Company. He influenced many people in the course of his work.

How to Establish Strong Business Ethics?

What will Japanese corporations have to do in order to establish strong business ethics? I would propose the following three points:

1. First, create a code of ethical business conduct and clarify ideas on the position of ethics in business management. Then show in concrete terms what actions are expected based on this code. Most of the recent unethical activities of Japanese companies have been conducted with the consent and tacit approval of high-level management. In this kind of environment, nothing will change. The top company officers must be the first to open their eyes to considerations of ethics and recognise their importance, and then put this understanding down in clear writing to transmit to all employees.

2. Second, a system must be erected for ensuring that the business code of ethics is being followed. The ethics officer in some US companies is probably an effective means for doing this. Another method is conducting regular surveys of employees (like in Johnson & Johnson) to learn exactly what is going on in the workplace.
3. Thirdly, ensuring everyday compliance with business ethics is a matter of the accumulation of many small innovations. TI, for instance, passes out an "ethics card" to each of its employees worldwide so that each employee can check his own actions against the standards written on the card. The standards are as follows: Is the action legal? Does it comply with our values? If you do it, will you feel bad? How will it look in the newspaper? If you know it's wrong, don't do it! If you're not sure, ask. Keep asking until you get an answer.

If employees are still unsure of what to do, the card gives the name and telephone number of the person they should contact to discuss the matter with. It cannot be denied that the "tacit understanding" in Japanese companies produces a sense of camaraderie and belonging within the company, increasing the sense of the company as a single unit and contributing to the overall strength of the business. However, considering the important role in society played by corporations, Japanese corporations must establish a code of business ethics in response to public criticism. To do so, they must put forth standards for everyday corporate behaviour that are straightforward and easy for anybody to understand.

Ethics and Conflicts

We define a conflict of interest as "a situation in which a person, such as a public official an employee or a professional, has a private or personal interest sufficient to appear to influence the objective exercise of his or her official duties." There are three key elements in this definition. First, there is a private or personal interest. Often this is a financial interest, but it could also be another sort of interest, say, to provide a special advantage to a spouse or child. Taken by themselves, there is nothing wrong with pursuing private or personal interests, for instance, changing jobs for more pay or helping your daughter improve her golf stroke.

The problem comes when this private interest comes into conflict with the second feature of the definition, an "official duty" – quite literally the duty you have because you have an office or act in an official capacity. As a professional, you take on certain official responsibilities, by which you acquire obligations to clients, employers, or others. These obligations are supposed to trump private or personal interests.

Third, conflicts of interest interfere with professional responsibilities in a specific way, namely, by interfering with objective professional judgment. A major reason clients and employers value professionals is that they expect professionals to be objective and independent. Factors, like private and personal interests, which either interfere or appear likely to interfere with objectivity, are then a matter of legitimate concern to those who rely on professionals – be they clients, employers, professional colleagues or the general public. So it is also important to avoid apparent and potential as well as actual conflicts of interests. An apparent conflict of interest is one in which a reasonable person would think that the professional's judgement is likely to be compromised. A potential conflict of interest involves a situation that may develop into an actual conflict of interest.

How do we determine if you are in a conflict of interest, whether actual, apparent or potential? The key is to determine whether the situation we are in is likely to interfere or appear to interfere with the independent judgement we are supposed to show as a professional in performing our official duties. A good test is the "trust test": Would relevant others (our employer, our clients, professional colleagues, or the general public) trust our judgement if they knew we were in this situation? Trust, in our opinion, is at the ethical heart or core of this issue. Conflicts of interest involve the abuse, actual or potential, of the trust people have in professionals. This is why conflicts of interest not only injure particular clients and employers, but also the whole profession by reducing the trust people generally have in professionals.

In fact, the "trust test" suggests one very good way of dealing with a conflict of interest: Reveal your private interest in the matter to the relevant parties. Often, if we let others know what might be influencing our judgement, they can be on their guard and not caught unawares.

But, sometimes, it is not enough to know that there is a particular private interest influencing a professional's judgement; the client, employer, etc., expects that the professional will stay out of such situations. So, the second way to avoid conflicts of interests is to absent yourself from decision-making or advice-giving if you have a private interest. In the case of potential self-dealing, the conscientious professional will say that she cannot be involved in a situation where She is both bidding on a government contract and deciding as a public servant who is awarded the contract. He will either step aside and completely (and, I mean, completely) absent himself from determining who gets the contract or refrain from bidding on such contracts in the first place – which is probably the wisest course of action.

It may take some skill and good judgement to recognise that we are in a conflict of interest situation. This is because private and personal interests can cloud a person's objectivity. So it may be a lot easier to recognise when others are in a conflict than when we are. This suggests that it may be useful to talk to a trusted colleague or friend when we are in doubt.

But once we recognise that we are in or are headed for a conflict of interest situation, the ethical responses are straightforward: Get out of the situation, or if we cannot, make known to all affected parties our private interest. These responses will preserve the trust essential to professional objectivity.

It is important to realise that avoiding conflicts of interest is only one part of being a conscientious professional. Another part is the difficult task of making choices when the ethics of the situation aren't clear or when there are good moral reasons for acting in diametrically opposing ways. This is typical in the case of whistle blowing, in which a duty of loyalty to a client or employer counsels confidentiality, but this conflicts with a duty to warn the public of a serious harm or danger.

Thus spoke Aurobindo while making comments on conflicts and humanity:[4]

> "In the conflict of the claims of society with the claims of the individual,. two ideal and absolute solutions confront one another. There is the demand of the group that the individual should subordinate himself more or less completely or even lose his independent existence in the community, the smaller must be immolated or self-offered to the larger unit. He must accept the need of the society as his own need, the desire of the society as his own desire; he must live not for himself but for the tribe, clan, commune or nation of which he is a member. The ideal and absolute solution from the individual's standpoint would be a society that existed not for itself, for its all-overriding collective purpose, but for the good of the individual and his fulfilment, for the greater and more perfect life of all its members. Representing as far as possible his best self and helping him to realise it, it would respect the freedom of each of its members and maintain itself not by law and force, but by the free and spontaneous consent of its constituent persons."

And, in the present balance of humanity, there is seldom any real danger of exaggerated individualism breaking up the social integration. There is continually a danger that the exaggerated pressure of the social mass by its heavy unenlightened mechanical weight may suppress or unduly discourage the free development of the individual spirit. For man in the individual can be more easily enlightened, made conscious and open to clear influences; man in the mass is still obscure, half-conscious, ruled by universal forces that escape its mastery and its knowledge.

Notes

1. Jerry Mander, "The Rules of Corporate Behaviour" in *The Case Against the Global Economy,* Ed. Jerry Mander and, Edwards Goldsmith, Sierra Book Club, 1996.
2. *Humanscape*, July 2000, in a personal interview to Nisha Susan Abraham.
3. Basant K. Lal, *Vedanta and the Contemporary Problem of Man's Estrangement in Indian Philosophical Systems,* The Ramakrishna Mission Institute of Culture, Kolkata, Pp. 34-45, Kolkata.
4. *The Future Evolution of Man – Sri Aurobindo,* Conclusion of Chapter 4 – "Standards of Conduct and Spiritual Freedom", Prepared by P.B. Saint-Hilaire, August 1962.

8

Consciousness, Morality and Responsibilities: The East and the West

I

In the light of the evolutionary doctrine, Aurobindo envisages a gradual transformation towards the divine. In his interpretation of evolution, the teleological motive for all terrestrial changes in living organisms is the emergencc of consciousness. In his system, the consciousness that appears first is embryonic and imperfect. It gradually evolves and finally reaches it apex in the human being. However, even in its highest elevation, the human being retains its bestial qualities, which act as a "pull of gravitation towards the original inertia and nescience". The human being is yet to evolve out of this gloomy cave of ignorance towards a more authentic being. Such a mode of existence could be the product only of the forthcoming stages of evolution. This concept is only slightly different from the earlier sub-continental notion that it is possible for the human being to gradually improve the human condition at different, successive phases of his life, and eventually liberate himself from the vicissitudes of materiality. According to Aurobindo, even at the present stage of existence, the human being can see the possibility of enriching his existence to a higher rank.

Hence, the human being has the essential desire to surpass his limitations. This impulse is fundamental to the very nature of humanity. The human consciousness must have a role in this transformation. Often, Aurobindo does not clearly state whether the human consciousness is active or passive in the leap to the next evolutionary stage. But he is quite confident that there is no reason for such a mutation to be impossible on the terrestrial level. He believes that since consciousness is concealed in living matter before its inception, the super-consciousness is similarly buried in the human being, waiting to be released. In his system, the mind is the highest dimension at the present stage of evolution above which is the super-mind, a stage of evolution of which existence is capable, but which it has not yet reached.

Aurobindo examines the present obstacles in the evolutionary process. Like the *rishis* who believed that reason is not sufficient to probe into the realm of sacred knowledge, he believes that reason does not arrive at the ultimate truth. But he admits that in spite of shortcomings, reason does have a justifiable role in explaining empirical reality to human beings and in expanding their cognitive field. Even religion becomes embodied in rigid and static formations. His attitude toward canons is not different from what the *rishis* declared: "Of what use is the *RgVeda* to one who does not know the Spirit from whom the *RgVeda* comes, and in whom all things abide?" Therefore, he argues, what the individual must find is an alternate answer to the evolutionary crisis, an answer in which "a total spiritual direction given to the whole life and the whole nature can alone lift humanity beyond Itself". This evolutionary step, undoubtedly, will require an exodus from all previous suppositions about human existence. To break the bondage of ignorance, the human being must find the secret that dwells in his heart. He argues that the nature of evolution is such that the concepts of good and evil change their meaning and value with the flow of time. Though the standards of conduct in society may be necessary in a given epoch, the values of behaviour are not eternally fixed. He pities the zealot who erects in vain his absolute standards and call upon all to be faithful to it without regard to consequences.

Aurobindo believes that the spiritual development of the human being is the progressive evolution of the inner reality contained in the human soul. The task of spiritual realisation is to heighten the consciousness of the soul and to build a more coherent life. He refutes the two main criticisms about the mystic. First, in answer to the claim that the mystic turns away from life, he asserts that the task of spirituality is not to resolve current problems, but to lay the foundation for the higher spiritual being that will overcome the problems of life once the spiritual nature of the human being develops sufficiently. Hence, for him, the challenge of spirituality is to create a new foundation for divine life, rather than to analyse the miseries of current human existence. Second, in answer to the claim that mystical knowledge is purely subjective, he points out that since truth is many sided, its differences will appear arbitrary until harmonised in a higher consciousness. He argues that that it is incorrect to demand only one system of ideas since variation lies in the essence of spiritual experience.

According to Aurobindo, the significance of spiritual transformation of the human being consists not only in his release from ignorance and bondage, but also in the recreation of temporal reality. He shows how this mutation will take place in three distinct phases: 1. psychic transformation; 2. spiritual transformation, and 3. super-mental transformation. Change is the psychic part in the human being and is necessary because it is the part that retains the human identity and is not limited by what is manifest in human activity. A psychic change can take place with the re-orientation of the spiritual for only sense of "a boundless self, a boundless light, boundless power, a boundless ecstasy" can open the vision of the psyche. This change can be brought about by a super-mental intervention in the terrestrial existence of the human being.

Aurobindo follows the sub-continental tradition in conceiving that there are three roads to the liberation of the soul. These three paths are: 1. The way of knowledge; 2. the way of devotion, and 3. the way of action. He believes that the synthesis of these three within the individual will enable the human being to attain the "composite perfect of the saint, the selfless worker and the man of spiritual knowledge" (Sri Aurobindo Birth Centenary Library, Vol. 26, *Sri Aurobindo on Himself*, pp. 95-97).

Aurobindo lays down the prerequisites for the transformation of the mind to the super-mind. While it is true that this transmutation cannot be completed without super-mental effort, conscious human effort is also necessary. First, the human being must become aware of the divine in him. Second, the human being must surrender his total being to the will of the divine. Third, the individual and the whole must unite to break down the walls that separate each other. According to him, this transformation takes place in a step-by-step process, which "can only be achieved when the substance of being is so steeped in the spiritual principle that all its movements are a spontaneous dynamism and a harmonised process of the spirit".

Aurobindo points out the limitations of analysing the super-mental nature because it escapes the human being, whose perspectives are circumscribed perspectives and whose knowledge is based upon a consciousness of the finite. With the evolution of the super-mind, there will appear the person "who has discovered his soul: He has found his self and lives in that, is conscious of it, has the joy of it; he needs nothing external for his completeness of existence". He is the gnostic being. This gnostic being will realise the oneness of the universe. The gnostic being will not feel any disharmony with the cosmic consciousness. While remaining the spiritual self, the gnostic being will be able to enter this world without sacrificing his unity with the ultimate. The relation between spirit and matter will be reversed, allowing a new interaction in which the spirit will attain absolute control of the total being. Cosmic joy will be the essence of the transformed nature. The gnostic being's nature will be the nature of the divine; hence, there will be compatibility between the impersonal and the personal. The nature of the gnostic being will be a spiritual self-nature, a self-flow of being, where freedom and order form a dialectic harmony. For the gnostic being, there is no conflict, no strife. Thus, no distinction can be drawn between the identity of the divine being and the identity of all beings.

The aim of the integral *yoga* philosophy is neither the repudiation of the material world nor the absolute approbation of material existence, but the discovery of the unity of nature and spirit. In Aurobindo's system, too, the highest aim is the being of one, without the renunciation of life in the world. Such a fulfilment of the consciousness, the urge for perfection, must not be confined to a few individuals, but must extend to the masses, leading to a new type of being that is "eternal, self-existing and inalienable". Aurobindo's evolutionary doctrine points to the conventional model of sub-continental thought, which holds that only a few may actually attain spiritualisation in life. According to him, the gnostic being will use his powers of greater consciousness for action, knowledge and devotion in a spontaneous way. The gnostic being will achieve a status exceeding the human level. He insists that this must not be confused with earlier notions of supermanhood. Gnostic consciousness will comprehend and espouse the infinite. Aurobindo concludes that the human being is on this quest for self-realisation and liberation through the evolution of his self (*The New Nation,* November 25 and December 2, 1988).

Aurobindo teaches that a descent of the higher principle is possible which will not merely release the spiritual self out of the world, but release it in the world, replace the mind's ignorance or its very limited knowledge by a supramental truth consciousness, which will be a sufficient instrument of the inner self and make it possible for the human being to find himself dynamically as well as inwardly and grow out of his still animal humanity into a diviner race. The psychological discipline of *yoga* can be used to that end by opening all the parts of the being to a conversion or transformation through the descent and working of the higher, still-concealed supramental principle.

This, however, cannot be done at once or in a short time or by any rapid or miraculous transformation. Many steps have to be taken by the seeker before the supramental descent is possible. Man lives mostly in his surface mind, life and body, but there is an inner being within him with greater possibilities to which he has to awaken – for it is only a very restricted influence from it that he receives now and that pushes him to a constant pursuit of a greater beauty, harmony, power and knowledge. The first process of *yoga* is therefore to open the ranges of this inner being and to live from there outward, governing his outward life by an inner light and force. In doing so, he discovers in himself his true soul, which is not this outer mixture of mental, vital and physical elements, but something of the reality behind them, a spark from the one divine fire. He has to learn to live in his soul and purify and orientate himself by its drive towards the truth. There can follow afterwards an opening upward and descent of a higher principle of the being. But even then it is not at once the full supramental light and force. For there are several ranges of consciousness between the ordinary human mind and the supramental truth consciousness. These intervening ranges have to be opened up and their power brought down into the mind, life and body. Only then can the full power.of the truth consciousness work in nature. The process of this self-discipline or *sadhana* is therefore long and difficult, but even a little of it is so much gained because it makes the ultimate release and perfection more possible.

There are many things belonging to older systems that are necessary on the way – an opening of the mind to a greater wideness and to a sense of the self and the infinite, an emergence into what has been called the cosmic consciousness, mastery over desires and passions; an outward asceticism is not essential, but the conquest of desire and attachment and a control over the body and its needs, greeds and instincts are indispensable. There is a combination of the principles of the old systems, the way of knowledge through the mind's discernment between reality and the appearance, the heart's way of devotion, love and surrender and the way of works turning the will away from motives of self-interest to the truth and the service of a greater reality than the ego. For the whole being has to be trained so that it can respond and be transformed when it is possible for that greater light and rorce to work in nature.

In this discipline, the inspiration of the Master, and in the difficult stages, his control and his presence are indispensable, for it would be impossible otherwise to go through it without much stumbling and error, which would prevent all chance of success. The Master is one who has risen to a higher consciousness and being and he is often regarded as its manifestation or representative. He helps by his teaching and still more by his influence and example, and also by a power to communicate his own experience to others.

This is Aurobindo's teaching and method of practice. It is not his object to develop any one religion or to amalgamate the older religions or to found any new religion – for any of these things would lead away from his central purpose. The one aim of his *yoga* is an inner self-development by which each one who follows it can in time discover the one self in all and evolve a higher consciousness than the mental, a spiritual and supramental consciousness which will transform and make divine human nature.

II

Edmund Husserl was a German philosopher who founded *phenomenology*. He was professor at the universities of Gottingen (1901-16) and Freiburg (1916-29). At first a mathematician, he became interested in the philosophy of Franz Brentano, whose concept of intention was applied to the philosophy of consciousness in the maxim: "All consciousness is consciousness of something."

Husserl combined his interests in mathematics, formal logic and psychology in his first book, *The Philosophy of*

Arithmetic, published in 1891. The properly phenomenological themes of his philosophy were first presented explicitly in his *Logical Investigations* (1900-01; English trans., 1970). In his 1907 lectures, "The Idea of a Phenomenology", published in English in 1964, and his book, *Ideas: General Introduction to Phenomenology* (1913; English trans., 1931), he proposed the methodological suspension of all judgements about the character and even about the existence of the objects of consciousness, in order to describe experience from the inside. That is, Husserl was concerned with what it meant for something to appear, or to be, a "phenomenon". He found it necessary to suspend judgement about the given reality of things, to "bracket" data or consciousness, in order to describe them. In this way imaginary objects could be examined as seriously as objective reality. Husserl concluded that consciousness is dependent upon the objects it considers.

Husserl's description of the consciousness of time, presented in *The Phenomenology of Inner Time-Consciousness* (1928; English trans., 1964), the revisions of his logical theory in *Formal and Transcendental Logic* (1929; English trans., 1969), his discussion of a person's experience of other minds in *Cartesian Meditations* (1931; English trans., 1960), and his later emphasis on the basic nature of humans' lived relationship with the world (*lebenswelt*) in *Experience and Judgment* (1939; English trans., 1973) have influenced philosophers in many different fields. His most famous pupil was Martin Heidegger, who transformed Husserl's relatively cognitive phenomenological method into an existentialism that dealt with the emotional and ethical significance of life as well as its perceptual, intellectual and logical structures.

There is a thin, blurred line separating phenomenology and existentialism. Edmund Husserl was the leading thinker in the Phenomenological Movement, influencing most future existentialists either directly or indirectly. Husserl's phenomenology was a descriptive analysis of subjective processes. He described it as the "intuitive study of essences".

According to Husserl, the goal of philosophy was to describe the data of consciousness without bias or prejudice, ignoring all metaphysical and scientific theories in order to accurately describe and analyse the data gathered by the human senses and the mind. The students of Husserl summarised phenomenology as the study of "the things themselves."

The pursuit of "essences" was to be accomplished in phenomenology via three techniques: phenomenological reduction, eidetic reduction and cognition analysis.

Phenomenological reduction, according to Husserl's teachings, is the exclusion from consideration of everything which is transcendent and anything else derived via scientific or logical inference. A phenomenologist would consider only what was immediately presented to consciousness. This is familiar to students of Jean-Paul Sartre, who suggested what you know of a person or item is all that you can evaluate. An object, even a person, is only what one sees and experiences of that object. The rest, Husserl suggested, was "bracketed out" from judgement. Husserl referred to this suspension of judgement as "epoché".

Eidetic reduction is the abstraction of essences. The essence abstracted via eidetic reduction is the intelligible structure of the phenomenon found in consciousness. The goal is to find the basic components of a phenomenon. For example, a chair might include the colour, the materials used, and the shapes present in the structure. We apply basic, platonic forms to all phenomena, according to Husserl. These basics allow us to communicate and describe a phenomenon with some accuracy, though this lessens the original phenomenon in some manner.

Returning to the example of colour, one knows there are component colours. If one thinks too much about the mixture of colours, the colour viewed is devalued. Green is green, according to Husserl, not a mixture of blue and yellow subtractives. The scientific knowledge of colour is the universal form: there are agreed upon mathematical representations of colour. Still, colour is a personal and subjective phenomenon, further complicated by differences in human senses, such as colour blindness.

Cognition analysis is the detailed comparison between the phenomenon as presented in consciousness and the universal form of the phenomenon. We, as humans, struggle to align our experience of colour with our scientific knowledge of colour. Phenomenology attempts to reconcile what humans experience with what humans suppose to know via theory. There is a distinction between the phenomenon as experienced and the cognition; Husserl compared "appearance" to "that which appears".

Husserl's Triad: Ego, Cogito, Cogitata

What phenomenologists consider important is that which can be experienced via the human senses. After reduction and abstraction, what remains is what an individual knows, regardless of the scientific or transcendental data. After removing the transcendental and the scientific, what remains is the "phenomenological residue" of the phenomenon. This residue exists in three forms: ego, cogito and cogitata.

Phenomenological ego is the stream of consciousness in which one acquires meaning and reality from the surrounding environment. Husserl considered it a great mystery and wonder that a group of beings was aware of its existence, in effect human consciousness is the phenomenological result of introspection. By observing that "I can touch and see my being", we recognise that we exist. The science proving we exist is not of value to human consciousness. The ego is always present, or nothing exists for the individual.

Cogito or cogitations comprise all the acts of consciousness, including doubting, understanding, affirming, denying, etc. The ego exists only as a result of these cogitations and these cogitations continue only as long as we are self-aware.

Cogitata are the subjects of thought or objects of consideration. One cannot deny or understand nothing – something must be under consideration for thought to occur. In the presence of nothing, there is no person, no individual.

Transcendental Idealism

"Everything which is and has reality for me, that is, for man, exists only in my own consciousness," Husserl stated. According to Husserl, through reduction, the phenomenological ego can become an observer of itself, aware of itself and self-conscious. Since we gain knowledge via this ego, we learn about the ego as we learn about the environment around us.

Humans presuppose that other egos exist. We assume that other humans are self-aware, with no proof of this since we cannot observe the thoughts of others – only their actions. Husserl sought a "community of selves" in which all were aware of each other. "I experience the world not as my own private world, but as an intersubjective world."

Since we learn about the world through observing external phenomena, and that is how we learn about ourselves, we in effect must learn about ourselves through others. Consider that you need a mirror to see yourself, you have no internal self-knowledge of your facial features. Likewise, you can only observe the results of your emotions and thoughts through the responses of other humans.

III

Martin Heidegger (1889-1996) began as a recognised authority in the phenomenological movement and became an existentialist with theistic leanings. Heidegger based his philosophy upon the "hermeneutics of existence" – or the science of existence. The "scientific" method was that of phenomenological reduction.

Heidegger saw the rise of modern technology as de-humanising man – a rather generalising Luddite view, but repeated with much insistence, so we assume that was the effect it had on him at least (obviously he didn't actually do any experiments, research or empirical studies to attempt to validate any of his generalisations). What did he actually want to do about the situation? Now this is really the crux of both the appeal and the emptiness of Heidegger because he did not actually want to do anything particularly practical but his poetic language calling to mind a time of farmers, shepherds, Greek gods, nature, community, yet used to describe anthropological/ontological structures rather than sociological ones, is his great appeal. Is it possible to cover the world – this harsh, industrial, inhuman world – with a language of nature, of high culture, of artistic beauty? Or perhaps, if we start thinking like Heidegger suggests (seeing ourselves as guardians – not exploiters, etc.), the world will begin to change, too. Rather like hoping that the pin-up posters with their enormous soft breasts that the workers cover their hard, oily machinery with will somehow change the nature of the machine.

Post-modernism uses the power of the consumer image – and the technology that reproduces that image – to create a different subjectivity. Heidegger cannot remain part of the old culture and has not the strength of vision to become part of the new one. He is the compost of philosophy, thought that has rotted.

What does Heidegger desire? The understanding of desire in Heidegger is itself best understood as the desire for truth being the sublimation of a repressed desire for a forbidden object. His later views, rejecting the will, concern with letting the being be, etc., may similarly be seen as (i) an expression of a contradiction in rejecting and exhibiting a desire for truth, the existence of a contradiction itself being a cypher for desire, and (ii) loss of an essential part of listening to the being – Heidegger is ignorant of ecstacy, frenzy, hallucination, punishment, fear, etc., as the mouth of the oracle of the being, and his frigidness is punished with ignorance.

A world-view must be able to match the other world-views with which it is competing; it must have a culture, a philosophy, a morality, etc., and be sufficiently deep enough to satisfy the intellectual. Marxism's success is not its truth, but because it comes near this ideal; similarly, Heidegger has appeal, albeit limited, because to contain the kernel of a whole world-view.

Dasein

According to Heidegger's writings, a human being – as opposed to human beings – comprises four components: concern, being-toward-death, existence and moods. Dasein is the act of "being there" in essence. Without being something, there is no existence.

Concern, or *sorge,* is the ability to care about the self, in relation to phenomena. Being-toward-death, or *sein zum tode,* represents the finite nature of life. This belief that death defines life complements the thought that G.-d does not exist, but is real. Existence, or *existenz,* represents knowing one is and is changing. Finally, moods, or *stimmungen,* are reactions to other beings, further allowing one to define the self.

Dasein requires choices and resulting actions to define the self. These choices allow for an almost unlimited combination of the components of being. Each choice represents a pivotal point in the individual's life – every choice, even the seemingly minor ones, contribute to the larger definition of self. Choices occur in relation to a timeline, universal and personal. These points in time became the topic of Heidegger's *Being and Time.*

Existence and Essence

As with Kierkegaard and Sartre, Heidegger believed the existence of a physical body preceded the essence of self. At some point in the development process, a being becomes aware that it exists. This pivotal point in time is when essence begins to form; the individual decides to acknowledge and embrace an essence at this moment.

Because man is the only known being in which essence and existence do not appear simultaneously, man is a unique creature on this planet. All things man creates have essence, or definition, before they exist. In other words, an individual thinks about a creation and its purpose before the creation exists.

Dasein Sorge

Dasein sorge was Heidegger's term for concern and caring about the self and its existence. When confronted with the world and other beings, the individual feels anxiety and dread. The world appears complex and unsafe – which it is. As a result, the human being, *dasein,* must care for itself as no one else can or will.

Taking care of the self is a sign that the individual recognises dangers in the universe. Recognising threats demonstrates an understanding of the physical self. It is reasonable to conclude that concern with the physical self precedes the awareness of concern for the emotional self. While a child might instinctively want human contact, it only understands the need for food and other basic physical needs.

Classes of Dasein Existence

Being there, *dasein* can be expressed in several fashions. The five modes of *dasein* described by Heidegger are: authenticity, inauthenticity, everydayness, averageness. and publicness. Authenticity represents a choice of self and achievement. All other modes represent a failing to embrace the individuality available to all people.

Inauthenticity results from business, preoccupation, excitement and other external forces. An inauthentic being is working to fit the definitions of others. Averageness takes hold when the individual no longer attempts to achieve and accepts a loss of differentiation. Everydayness represents a person no longer changing or making choices, but the individual might still be different from others. Many achievers become everyday when they no longer attempt to excel.

Publicness is the complete loss of self for a public image. The individual conforms to preconceptions and opinions. Unlike the celebrity with one achievement, this individual repeats the same achievement over and over, thereby withdrawing from independence. An example would be an artist with one style of expression, repeated with minor variations to please others. By avoiding the new, the different, the individual ceases to create and define a self.

Sein zum Tode: Being Toward Death

The only proof that an individual understands existence is the understanding and acceptance of death. While a child can understand the physical need for food, the known consequences of not eating are limited to hunger and illness. Death is a complex concept, beyond the grasp of an immature existence.

The moment one accepts death is the point when essence is brought into focus. Knowing that life is finite reinforces the importance of all further decisions. Poor choices result in the "existential guilt" of failure. For the existentialist, the worst of natural sins is a failure to define the self using free will. Guilt cannot be avoided, however, because all individuals fail to take some action, to make some choices.

Desire to Be

Though life is filled with dread that the universe is not safe and guilt that life is never complete, the human being has a desire to exist and define the self. The pursuit of authenticity is constant for the existentialist. While it cannot be perfected, as we coexist with other beings, individuals must work to define themselves.

Individuals make decisions knowing that others might try to change the universe around them. Business is unavoidable, as is a public role in society. Only the most dedicated existential being can rise above these challenges to define the self without regard to others.

Contemporary Understanding of Being/Power

Heidegger understands our current understanding of being by looking at one of its greatest achievements, scientific research. His account of modern scientific practices is similar to Thomas Kuhn's in *The Structure of Scientific Revolutions*. What Heidegger calls "research" resembles what Kuhn calls "normal science". Research operates by setting up a "total" interpretation of some region of reality and then attempts to show that the anomalies that emerge can be fitted into this total account. Heidegger's researchers, like Kuhnian normal scientists, keep busy by taking for granted that their general plan is correct; that the anomalies it reveals have no truth to tell, so that in the end, they must all be brought under the projected total order.

Thus scientific research is made possible by Descartes' unthought fully focussed in Kant, that rationality consists in human beings imposing a total, systematic order on all that is. Heidegger calls this totalising the understanding of being "technological".

Like many current critics of the modern age, Heidegger at first failed to distinguish the modern epoch that was coming to an end from the beginning of the post-modern epoch. Thus, he was for a time under the illusion that the danger of technology was still that man was dominating everything and exploiting all beings for his own satisfaction. As if man were a subject in control, and the objectification of everything was the problem. He says in 1940:

> Western history has now begun to enter into the completion of that period we call the *modern*, and which is defined by the fact that man becomes the measure and the center of beings. Man is what lies at the bottom of all beings; that is, in modern terms, at the bottom of all objectification and representability.

By 1946, however, Heidegger saw that the modern understanding of being was coming to an end. The exploitation and control was not the subject's doing, and "man" never was anything but an effect of other forces.

> Even this, that man becomes the subject and the world the object, is a consequence of technology's nature establishing itself, and not the other way around.

In his final analysis of technology, Heidegger is critical of those who, still caught in the subject/object picture, think that technology is dangerous because it embodies instrumental reason. Modern technology, he insists, is "something completely different and therefore new". Heidegger describes the hydroelectric power station on the Rhine as his paradigm technological device because for him electricity is the paradigm technological stuff. He says:

> The revealing that rules throughout modern technology has the character of a setting-upon, in the sense of a challenging-forth. That challenging happens in that the energy concealed in nature is unlocked, what is unlocked is transformed, what is transformed is stored up, what is stored up is, in turn, distributed, and what is distributed is switched about *ever anew*.

But we can see now that electricity is not a perfect example of technological stuff because it ends up finally turned into light, heat or motion to satisfy some subject's desire. Heidegger's intuition is that treating everything as standing reserve or, as we might better say, resources, makes possible "endless" disaggregation, redistribution, and reaggregation "for its own sake". As soon as he sees that information is truly endlessly transformable, Heidegger switches to computer manipulation of information as his paradigm.

The goal of technology, Heidegger then tells us, is more and more flexibility and efficiency simply for its own sake. There is no longer, as there was in Kant, an onto-theological centre that provides a goal for all activity. There is ordering, but no orderer. Heidegger says:

> Everywhere everything is ordered to stand by, to be immediately at hand, indeed to stand there just so that it may be on call for a further ordering. Whatever is ordered about in this way has its own standing. We call it the standing reserve (*bestand, i.e., resources*).

Heidegger seems to waver on the question whether, as technology reaches its final stage, it will accentuate subjects and objects or eliminate them.

> The subject-object relation thus reaches, for the first time, its pure "relational", i.e., ordering, character in which both the subject and the object are sucked up as standing-reserves. That does not mean that the subject-object relation vanishes, but rather the opposite: it now attains to its most extreme dominance.

In the end, however, he seems clearly to hold that technology can treat people and things as resources to be enhanced without setting meaning-giving subjects over against objectified things. A year after the previous remark about subjects and objects reaching extreme dominance, Heidegger appears to retract his view about objects at least, in his observation that nature has become "a system of information" and a modern airliner is not an object at all, but just a flexible and efficient cog in the transportation system. Passengers are presumably not autonomous subjects either, but resources recruited by the tourist industry to fill the planes. Heidegger concludes: "Whatever stands by in the sense of standing-reserve no longer stands over against us as object."

Heidegger's basic idea was that western human beings are essentially disclosers of a series of total worlds. One way to open new worlds is to reconfigure the practices by making marginal practices central and central practices marginal. This would result in a new understanding of being focussed in a new god. So we can see why, for Heidegger, the way Kant's world picturing has worked itself out as "total" mobilisation and so tending towards the incorporation of all marginal practices, is the greatest danger. It eliminates those very practices on the basis of which new worlds can be disclosed and dooms us to the eternal return of the same.

For Heidegger, the gathering of local practices around things such as a jug of wine or a family meal produces temporary, self-enclosed, local worlds that resist the totalising and dispersing effects of the flexible and efficient ordering demanded by the technological understanding of being. Thus, cultivating what Albert Borgmann calls focal practices gives a new centre, or better new centres to our lives. Human beings still have the job of world disclosing and preserving, now called dwelling on earth

There is, nonetheless, an important kind of resistance these two thinkers share. Thinking the history of being, for Heidegger, and the genealogy of regimes of power, for

Foucault, opens a space for critical questioning by showing that our understanding of reality need not be defined by techno/bio power – that we need not be dominated by the drive to order and optimise everything. They both show that we had a different relation to being and to power once, which suggests that we could have that relation again. Thus, an understanding of our historical condition weakens the hold our current understanding has on us and makes possible disengagement from the direction our practices are taking. Both thinkers were once prophets of the dawning of a new world, but both gave up that stance. They both came to share Heidegger's modest claim that:

> The thinking in question remains unassuming because its task is only of a preparatory, not of a founding character. It is content with awakening a readiness in man for a possibility whose contour remains obscure, whose coming remains uncertain.

When he was thinking of modes of resistance to the technological understanding of being, Heidegger came to think that there was an essential antagonism between a unified understanding of being and local worlds. Of course, he always realised that there would be an antagonism between the style set up by a cultural paradigm and things that could only be brought out in their ownness in a style different from the dominant cultural style. Such things would inevitably be dispersed to the margins of the culture. There, they will shine in contrast to the dominant style, but will have to resist being considered irrelevant or even wicked. But if there is a single understanding of being, even those things that come into their own in the dominant cultural style will be inhibited as things. Already in his essay "Thing", Heidegger goes out of his way to point out that even though the original meaning of "thing" in German is a gathering to discuss a matter of concern to the community, in the case of the thing thinging, the gathering in question must be self-contained. The focal occasion must determine which community concerns are relevant rather than the reverse.

Given the way local worlds establish their own internal coherence that resists any imposition from outside there is bound to be a tension between the glorious cultural paradigm that establishes an understanding of being for a whole culture and the humble inconspicuous things. The shining of one would wash out the shining of the others. The tendency toward one unified world would impede the gathering of local worlds. Given this tension, Heidegger abandoned in a late seminar what he had considered up to then his crucial contribution to philosophy, the notion of a single understanding of being and its correlated notion of the ontological difference between being and beings. He remarks that "from the perspective of appropriation it becomes necessary to free thinking from the ontological difference". He continues: "From the perspective of appropriation (letting-presence) shows itself as the relation of world and thing, a relation which could in a way be understood as the relation of being and beings. But then its peculiar quality would be lost." What presumably would be lost would be the self-enclosed local character of things. It follows that as mortal disclosers of worlds in the plural, the only comprehensiveness we can hope to achieve is our openness to dwelling in many worlds and the capacity to move among them. Only such a capacity allows us to accept Heidegger's criticism of technology and still have a genuinely positive relationship with it.

The moral seems to be that when one is looking for marginal practices that could support resistance to the dominant regime of power, rather than thinking of resistance as a new regime that is dawning or a new god that can save us, one should think of the marginal as what is outside power. It is precisely not power but things and selves which will be what one studies.

IV

Swami Vivekananda had the foresight to see all these mental and physical problems and warned us against all obstacles. His definite instruction was: "Before flooding India with political and socialistic ideas, deluge the country with religious ideas but this instruction was thrown to the air by our leaders who had in the meantime chosen to make politics their chief instrument." Knowing all their facts, Vivekananda turned to "history and reason" only in search of his instrument, rejecting all high-sounding doctrines of revolutions. He declared: "I am no preacher of any momentary social reform. I am not trying to remedy evils, only to ask you to go forward and complete the practical realisation of the scheme of human progress that has been laid out in the most perfect order of out ancestors. I only ask you to work more and more for the. The Vedantic ideal of solidarity of man and his inborn divine nature".

He wrote one should move towards total freedom in the physical, intellectual and spiritual spheres. If the social system stands in one's way in this respect, the system should be immediately destroyed. In the path of the development of manifestation of human excellence, there are three obstacles: *adhyatmika, adhibhautika* and *adhidaivika. Adhyatmika* obstacles are due to psychological limitations imposed by one's instincts. *Adhibhautika* obstacles are forces of external nature and *adhidaivika* obstacles are expressed in the form of antagonistic social conditions and systems. The aim of revolution is to eradicate all these forces, to win over the three obstacles so that men may develop themselves. In the political field, Swamiji spoke to give power to the masses, not to any group or individual. He even discarded the role of the benevolent ruler: "Even if the kings be of as godlike nature as that of Yudhistira, Ramachandra, Dharma Ashok or Akbar under whose benign rule the people enjoyed safety and prosperity, and were looked after with paternal care by their rulers, the hand of him who is always fed by another gradually loses the power of taking the food to his mouth. His power of self-preservation can never become fully manifest who is always protected in every respect of another. Even the strongest youth remains but a child if his parents always look him after as a child. Being always governed by kings of godlike nature to whom is life the whole duty of protecting and providing for the people they can never get any occasion for understanding the principles of self government. Such a nation being entirely dependent on the king for everything and never caring to exert itself for the common good or for self-defence becomes gradually destitute of inherent energy and strength. If this state of dependence and protection continues long, it becomes the cause of the destruction of the nation, and its ruin is not far to seek. So the aim of revolution, according to Swamiji, is "salvation of the people by the people". In the sphere of economics, he was for equal distribution of wealth and not far accumulation of wealth like the Vaishya rule.

Swamiji stresses on social revolution along with cultural revolution. History proved Swamiji's view as a better one. Mere political revolution, even with an economic one, may bring Hitler, Khomeini and Pol Pot. Unless there is a cultural change, mere change of rulers and mode of production will not help much. According to Swamiji, revolution is a continuous and conscious process to make society better and for this, Swamiji placed his faith in the young generation.

He says: "The modern generation, they will work out the whole problem like lions. I have formulated the idea and have given my life to it. If I do not achieve success, some better one will come after me to work it out, and I shall be content to struggle. The problem you have is to give to the masses their rights. Give them their rights, and let them stand on their rights."

The young, the energetic, the strong, the well-built, the intellectual young men do not look up to the rich and great men who have money. The poor did all the great and gigantic work of the world. You, poor men... come up, you can do everything and you must do everything. Be steady, and above all be pure and sincere to the backbone. Have faith in your destiny. You young men ... are to work out the salvation of India ... I believe in it as I believe in my own body and my soul. Therefore, my heart goes to you young men. ... It depends upon you who have no money, because you are poor, therefore you will work. Because you have nothing, therefore you will be sincere. Because you are sincere, you will be ready to renounce all that is. This is your mission in life, this is my mission in life.

"In India, we have always been governed by kings, kings have made all our laws. Now the kings are gone and there is no one to make a move. The government dares not; it has to fashion its ways according to the growth of public opinion. It takes quite a long time to make healthy strong public opinion, which will solve its own problems, and in the interim, we shall have to wait. The whole problem of social reform, the tyranny of a minority is the worst tyranny that the world ever sees. A few men who think that certain things are evil will not make a nation move. Why does not the nation move? First educate the nation, create your legislative body and then the law will be forthcoming. First create the power, the sanction from which the law will spring. The kings are gone, where is the new ..... the power of the people? Bring it up. Therefore, even for social reform, the first duty is to educate the people and you will have to wait till the time comes."

Thus, first educate the nation, create the legislative body, and then the law will come. Therefore, even for social reform, the first duty is to educate the people so that they may be able to solve their own problems. Until that is done, all the ideal reforms will remain ideals only. And to give the people secular education, we have to follow the plan laid down by our ancestors, that is to bring all the ideals slowly down among the masses. Raise them slowly to equality. Impact even secular knowledge through religion. One must raise oneself by one's own exertions – this holds well in all spheres. We help them to help themselves. The moment they will come to understand their own condition and feel the necessity of help and improvement, know that your work is taking effect and is in the right direction. Then leave the peasant and labourers to look to their own problems.

Wisdom, knowledge, wealth, men, strength, power and whatever else nature gathers and provides us with, are all only for diffusion, when the moment for need is at hand.

If the society is weak and debilitated, it silently suffers all ill treatment at the hands of the governing body, and as the natural consequence, both the ruler and his people go down and fall into the most degraded state and thus become an easy prey to any nation stronger than themselves. Where the society is healthy and strong, there soon follows a fierce contest between the ruler and his subjects and the bureaucratic paraphernalia become like curio-objects preserved in museum galleries.

Strength is the medicine which the poor must have when tyrannised over by the rich. The lower classes are gradually awakening to this fact and making a united front against this determined to exact their legitimate due. In India, the masses will start awakening slowly, but it is a good sign because when the masses wake up, they will come to understand their oppression. It is they who have introduced civilisation amongst them and it is they who will pull it down. Therefore, try to rouse the three lower classes from slumber by imparting learning and culture to them. When they will awaken and waken one day they must, they also will not forget their good services to the poor and will remain grateful to them.

Considering the toiling masses, Marx considered the industrial workers as the harbinger of the revolution, but Vivekananda said that the youth would lead the path to change society. In China, Mao-Tse-Sung called mainly the youth to launch the Cultural Revolution. Milovan Djilas, the noted scholar of Yugoslavia, considered the combined front of the youth and the intellectuals as vanguards of revolution. Swamiji called the youth for revolution as to him, the youth is the genuine revolutionary class. If we look at history, we find that he was totally aware of social mobility and the inherent propensities in considering the youth as a genuine revolutionary class. The fall of the Shah in Iran, the Cultural Revolution in China, the struggle of Bangladesh, the Naxalite movement in India are all moving incidents in recent history.

The youth is by nature anti-establishment. This characteristic is seen at home as a generation gap, then it spreads when the youth goes to college and university. They are always dissatisfied with the established pattern, whether social or political. This very nature makes them first rebels and, when they get a concrete idea, revolutionaries. Swami Vivekananda called the youth to act as a catalyst among the masses. He did not like to see any group or party set up its firm leadership, rather he wanted collective action because leadership can always be captured by a man like Pol Pot, Khomeini or Idi Amin. So Swamiji wanted to start a movement which would usher in a renaissance in society. This revolution of thought, a radical change in spirit and outlook, would awaken the people to understand the objective situation, the social reality and the dynamics of social change.

In India, the masses only hope because the new order of things is the salvation of the people by the people. Swamiji asked the youth to work like a catalyst among the masses, to bring up the power of the people as the preparation for revolution.

The service to be done by the youth for our lower classes is to give them education, to develop their lost individuality. This is a great task for our youth. They are to be given ideas, their eyes are to be opened to what is going on in the world around and then they will work out their own salvation. Of course, it takes time, because to make a healthy, strong public opinion is not an easy task. Swamiji also said that man should grow in three spheres, i.e., physical, mental and spiritual. For physical growth, one needs food, clothing, housing, etc. Through education, one grows in the mental sphere. But growth of spirituality requires something more. With the help of science, technology and political philosophy, men have acquired objective freedom. But unless there is growth in the spiritual sphere, unless there is subjective freedom, men will use their objective freedom for their self-centred activities. Man is not only a social being, but also has his own individual existence. Unless this individual existence is manifested, there will be no real growth, he will work like a machine as a sheep in its flock. The existing world-views and self-views lay stress on physical and mental growth. Without subjective freedom, objective freedom has no lasting effects and it will bring about a crisis of identity among men and women. This point was very pertinently raised by Fromm (1942). Hence, men start feeling isolated, which drives them to devotion and submission to the powerful state organisation. Thus, social change results from the dynamic adoption of human nature to the structure of society. Changing social conditions result in the change of social character, which then gives rise to new ideas.

Swamiji advocated the spread of education, people's participation in social action and the uplift of women for the them, which is now accepted in all parts of the globe. Vivekananda was convinced through his historical studies that the future belonged to the common man, the masses and the labouring people. In a prophetic manner, as we have seen above, he said, "The upper classes of India – disappear in the void. Let new India arise in your place. Let her arise out of the peasant's cottage... out of the huts of the fishermen, the cobbler, the sweeper... lets her emanate from the factory, from the marts and markets." He was the only 19th century thinker who wanted leadership that grows from the masses. He had no faith in the upper class elites – "they are more dead than alive", he said. He foresaw that they would attempt to thrive on the misery of the people and, taking advantage of their ignorance, they would monopolise power once they attained power with the help of the masses. Hence he laid his faith on the masses only and declared that India's only hope lay in the masses. And he was quite sure that the solution of the problem of the masses was education. They have many grave problems, but none that cannot be solved by that magic word, "education". "Education, education and education above all," he said emphatically. Therefore he chalked out a programme of mass education and it was a concrete programme. Not only did he state the goals, but also the means of execution of the plan. His chief aim was to awaken the masses. He wanted to accomplish this with the message of the *Vedanta*, the message that everyone has the same potential to be great and good, and for this purpose, he wanted to organise the youth, the self-sacrificing youth and, above all, he emphasised character building. "The education that does not bring out strength of character, a spirit of philanthropy and the courage of the lion – is it worth the name?" he asked. "We want that education by which character is framed, strength of mind is increased, the intellect is expanded and by which one can stand on one's own feet." He was convinced that the enlightened masses composed of individuals with strong character, courage and manliness would do the rest to revolutionalise society. Coming to the second point, i.e., people's participation it was found that when panchayats and cooperatives were formed, they were basically "top-bottom" and not based on grassroots people. It was centralisation in the garb of decentralisation. Vivekananda observed that in Indian history, the grassroots remained in the hands of the people at the village level. In order to adopt a "bottom-top" model, we have to examine the unique nature of community participation. Vivekananda emphasised this factor in his letters, "every village there should be an in-built system, a core existence, an indigenous centre that takes care of the village and through which the villagers work together." Thus, the involvement of people in the process of development is required from the stage of decision-making to its evaluation. Secondly, to help them to build their own support system and also to help them to be able to share substantially in development efforts, mobilisation of local resources is an important task. This can be done by voluntary labour and by developing active sharing habits. This helps them to have a village bank as well as a grain bank to help them in times of distress. Noted economist Prof. Amartya Sen pointed out that since food and other commodities are not distributed freely, people's consumption depends on their "entitlements", that is on the bundle of goods over which they can establish ownership through production and trade using their own men. Famines are initiated by severe loss of entitlements of one or more occupation groups, depriving them of the opportunity to consume food. He prescribed further that public employment with cost wages could be an effective method. Offering public employment to potential famine victims can re-create lost purchasing power and prevent starvation. He suggested that the political framework of democracy and an uncensored press can make a substantial contribution to this, but it also calls for activism on the part of the public. Here lies the essence of Vivekananda. The villagers are to be motivated to take on their own responsibilities. In this way, they will themselves start projects in the fields of education, health, employment, housing, agriculture, etc. At the same time, all the villagers are to be involved in solving community problems. Thus, it will help them to build a community based society, where people, irrespective of caste, colour of creed, will participate.

An Example of Grounded Responsibility

Shiv Shankar Chakravarty, a social activist of international reputes and the director of the Lokashiksha Parishad, Ramakrishna Mission, narrated: "In Kolkata, when the slum-dwellers of Rambagan area came up with their successful projects in education, self-employment, housing, sanitorium, etc., it was an eye opener for the middle class educated elites of that locality. The example set by the poor taught others that they can also solve their problems, instead of depending on the government and other agencies." He went further: "Take the case of the Arapanch group of villages in West Bengal. The cluster of fourteen villages has 1950 families, the total population being 10,618 – mostly SC/ST communities. The Ramakrishna Mission started its work here in 1978. After fourteen years in 1992, the percentage of literacy went up to 85 per cent in 1978, 90 per cent of the people were below the poverty line. Malnutrition has been completely eradicated. The child mortality rate has gone down, the status of the families has shot up, there are no beggars in any of these villages; the community has small savings and grain banks and can deal with many of their problems without depending on assistance from outside."

Thus, to initiate development based on local people's participation is the call of the hour as envisaged by Vivekananda in his writings. Coming to the final point, i.e., uplift of women as a part of an effective economic programme, we find that Vivekananda concentrated on efforts to develop a full-fledged philosophy of equality – equality between men and women, between the privileged and the underprivileged in society. For securing the complete emancipation of women this was urgently needed because for centuries, priests have harped on the doctrine of inequality.

Vivekananda has shown very clearly that spirituality also degenerates and makes room for the worst kind of privileges and tyranny and then it is materialism which rescues the oppressed masses. No other protagonist of religion has ever conceded that credit to materialism. At the same time, he has very ably shown that spirituality rescues people from the savage strifes, class wars and conflicts resulting from materialism. He points out that the world would be destroyed had not spirituality come to the rescue when materialism fully grasped society.

In recent years, Sorokin offered a theory of social change akin to that of Vivekananda. According to him, there are three different socio-cultural patterns which succeed one another in a rhythmic manner. These are: 1. ideational, 2. idealistic, and 3. sensate (Fig. 8.1). The ideational pattern is characterised by the predominance of spirituality and transcendentalism. The sensate pattern is characterised by the predominance of materialism and the idealistic pattern is a mixture of the two. Sorokin's view confirms to that of Vivekananda in respect of the nature of the class struggle. Both uphold that struggle for privileges among the different classes are most intense in a period of sensate or materialistic culture. Explaining the point, Sorokin adds: "In a developed sensate mentality, every day begins with a fight for maximum share of happiness and prosperity. This often leads to conflicts and often results in revolts, wars and class struggles over taxation, which ruins security and in the long run makes economic prosperity

Figure 8.1

Sorokin's Model

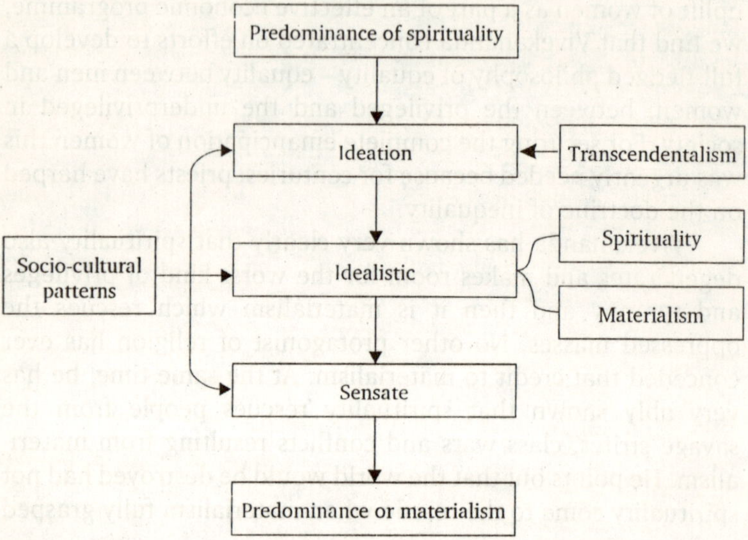

Reference: As quoted in the book edited by Das Gupta, Santwana, *Vivekananda: The Prophet of Human Emancipation,* Kolkata.

impossible. A new dynamic has to be found in consonance with the ultimate values of socialism. The ideals are eluding the socialistic movements in India because the approach is faulty. A socialist society is one in which the individual is prepared voluntarily to subordinate his own interest to the larger interest of society. Therefore, what is needed is not a dynamics based on conflicts of interests, but based on the values of the society. Vivekananda discovered a way of developing mass movements through internal change in man, mass moral revolutions. The world would be justified in expecting our country to have set an example in this respect. Wealth can be distributed by law, but shared only voluntarily. Distribution of wealth may be an uncertain step towards socialism, but sharing of wealth is real and full socialism. The fizzled out political ideology, "power money" managing groups of "narco-dollar" camp-followers only triggered off, in the name of social movements, a series of terrorism, intimidations and communal frenzies from the Jhelum to the Cape, tearing the country apart. Even a true revolution that is violent is neither swift nor sure. It takes a long time, sometimes centuries, for a violent revolution to succeed, and when it does, the aims of the revolution are thrust into the distant future. Thus the central point to be stressed in this connection is the question of values. Looked at from that standpoint, it should not be difficult, not only to chalk out the course for the future, but also to achieve a consensus of public opinion behind the endeavour to reconstruct a new society.

Summing up all the philosophical insights from the West and the East, we note that Husserl is generally associated with the modem development of phenomenology (a term he coined) as he attempted to create out of it a pure, non-empirical science. Husserl's focus was simply to study the nature of consciousness and how a conscious person could be conscious of their own consciousness. Thus, he criticised traditional attempts to understand the use of language through experience, arguing that naturalism was of no value and that insight was the best method to use here. This is true of the ethical practices in business as well because a manager should behave in such a way that gives the insights of that of an enlightened leader so that he could lead his team towards empowering them.

On the other hand, Martin Hiedegger felt that just as humans have progressively limited the being of the natural objects around them, they too have acquired a progressively limited character or being. While we have come to think that we encounter only ourselves in the world, in truth, however, precisely nowhere does man today any longer encounter himself Modern technology, in Heidegger's view, is the highest stage of misrepresentation of the essence of being human. So, we have to match machine with man in a very proportionate and prudent manner so that technology should not outwit mankind and the being-self.

Aurobindo never thought of spirituality as a solitary personal ascent to some celestial height. He saw no dichotomy between the spiritual and the worldly. Much of what he says has important relevance for our times. The century that is coming to an end has been a tumultuous one. Never before in history has time been so crowded with events.

What is indispensable is a readiness to shake off the puerile tricks of ego – a collective aspiration for transcendence into a meaningful existence. Aurobindo's optimism, based on a clear analysis of the adventure of human consciousness through the ages of ignorance – groping for "God, Light, Freedom, Bliss and Immortality" – and his vision of a new humanity, enrich our travails and struggles with a certain justification that nothing else seems to provide.

Hence, the concepts of "unity in diversity" and "*karmayoga*" of Vivekananda surface in the teachings of some great seers who have fully controlled their minds. To see the unifying self in all the diverse groups and serve the self in them all is the true meaning of *karmayoga*. However, the social workers and organisations do not take such broad view in their activities. In fact, there is no absolute need of an organisation to carry out *yoga* of selfless action. In whatever field one has chosen to work, or indeed is forced to work, that activity can be sublimated to the higher position of *yoga*. A clerk or an officer in an whatever field one has chosen to work, or indeed is forced to work, that activity can be sublimated to the higher position of *yoga*. A clerk or an officer in an office can think of serving the people in the queue outside his window by effectively attending to their needs and solving their problems; a farmer or a labourer can similarly take the worshipful attitude towards mother earth or temple of the factory. Such a conscious and deliberate attitude towards work as "worship" is the remedy for the feeling of estrangement and corruption.

Building of such an attitude, and a society, is possible, but it depends upon the will of the people, both holding high offices and ordinary folks without political or economical clout. Of course, the values trickle from the one who has cultivated and stored them in his/her personality. Thus, it is necessary and imperative that everyone struggles to imbibe and express values of selflessness, compassion, truthfulness and generosity in his character in howsoever small degree it may be possible for him. This is essential because unless we see the values as personified in someone else we cannot understand their utility. We see that the value-based life is calm and serene, without agitation and restlessness, pure and respectful, and thus try to seek the same for us also. Hence, it becomes essential to broadcast the beneficial impact of virtues on the individual and the society as a whole. In course of time, the truth is sure to blossom in the life of true *karmayogi* that all values have their source at the highest truth, the *atman*, residing in every heart.

Further Reading

Ackerman, Bruce, *Social Justice in the Liberal State*, Yale University Press, New Haven, Connecticut, 1980; and "Why Dialogue", *Journal of Philosophy 86*, No. 1, 1989, pp. 5-22, 155-56.

Benhabib, Seyla, *Situating the Self*, Routledge, Chapman & Hall, New Year, 1992, pp. 23-67.

Board of Education of Westside Community Schools v. Mergans 493 U.S. 182, 110 S.Ct. 2356 (1990).

Complete Works of Swami Vivekananda, Vol. IV, p. 443, Vol. VII, p. 149.

Darling-Hammond, Linda, "Valuing Teachers: The Making of a Profession", *Teachers College Record 87*, No. 3, 1985, 205-18.

Friedman, M., *Capitalism and Freedom*, University of Chicago Press, Chicago, 1962; J.E. Chubb and T.M. Moe, *Politics, Markets and America's Schools*, The Brookings Institution, Washington, D.C., 1990; and *The School-Choice Controversy,* Ed. J.W. Skillen, Baker Books, Grand Rapids, Michigan, 1993.

Gimmler, Antje, *The Discourse Ethics of Jürgen Habermas*, University of Marburg.

Habermas, Jürgen, *Moral Consciousness and Communicative Action*, Trans. Christian Lenhardt and Shierry Weber Nicholsen, The MIT Press, Cambridge, Massachusetts, 1990, pp. 66, 89.

Habermas, Jürgen, *Justification and Application: Remarks on Discourse Ethics*, The MIT Press, Cambridge, Massachusetts, 1993, p. 150.

Kuhn, Thomas, *The Structure of Scientific Revolutions,* University of Chicago Press, Chicago, 1970).

Lee v. Weisman 112 S.Ct. 2649 (1992), 2686.

MacIntyre, Alasdair, "Relativism, Power and Philosophy" in *After Philosophy, End or Transformation?*, Ed. Kenneth Baynes, James Bohman, and Thomas McCarthy, The MIT Press, Cambridge, Massachusetts, 1989, pp. 385-411.

MacIntyre, Alasdair, *After Virtue,* University of Notre Dame Press, Notre Dame, Indiana, 1981, p. 175.

Prangle, Lorraine Smith and Thomas Prangle, *The Learning of Liberty*, The University Press of Kansas, Lawrence, Kansas, 1993.

Rawls, John, *A Theory of Justice*, Harvard University Press, Cambridge, Massachusetts, 1971, pp. 520-29.

Taylor, Charles, *Multiculturalism and the Politics of Recognition*, Princeton University Press, Princeton, New Jersey, 1992, pp. 32, 67.

Sorokin, P. A., *Social and Cultural Dynamics* (abridged), London, 1978, ch. 35.

9

Spirituality at Work: Reflections and Lessons for a Better Future

Western culture, specifically the Euro-American mindset, for the past several hundred years, has depicted life as being composed of polar opposites in competition with each other: us/them, masculine/feminine, god/devil, sacred/secular. Many other cultures do not make these distinctions, especially between the sacred and the secular. These other cultures do not divide life into two separate spheres. Life is whole, of one piece. Life includes the opposites in a creative, vital and life-giving tension.

From this perspective then, there is not one set of rules and values brought to work and another set operational in other parts of life. If the connection or bridge can be made, this life would be of one piece. Our work and the way we work could truly be said at best to be spiritual, and at minimum to contain a spiritual dimension. Spirituality would permeate every aspect of this integrated life.

Spirituality

A hard word to define. Just hearing the word can make us uncomfortable at times (like fingernails Screeching on a blackboard), especially when we hear the words being used by someone to describe a perspective about life vastly different from our own. Spirituality is a very broad concept. It includes everything from ashrams to Zoroastrianism. And, spirituality is viewed as vague, mysterious and even phony by sceptics.

Are we aware of the spiritual dimensions of our daily tasks and life? Do these tasks serve, support, bring joy, create beauty, reconcile, renew, challenge and comfort, nurture, heal... all whom they touch? Work becomes fully spiritual when it touches both the giver and receiver in these ways.

Work of this kind has purpose beyond the pay cheque, beyond work tasks being ends in themselves. Work of this kind truly serves, supports, brings joy. When this happens, and even better when we become aware that it is happening or has happened, an important vital and mysterious spiritual connection is forged between personal fulfilment and making a contribution to the greater social good. Work, and its meaning for us, transcends the individual, the merely personal. Meaning is found that goes to the core and depth of our being. Meaning is found that satisfies, renews and sustains. Frederick Buechner has described that when this core and depth are struck, our deep gladness and the world's deep hunger meet.

If we do not consider that our work has a spiritual dimension, perhaps it is because we do not view work from a spiritual perspective. Perhaps, we try to separate life into two spheres, one sacred and one secular with no overlap, with no integration. Perhaps we seldom view our work or life as sacred because our daily tasks seem so routine, dehumanised and dehumanising, so minute, so unnecessary, that we see nothing of value in them for ourselves or others beyond the activity.

Good Work

Principle-centred business is concerned with the usual bottomline line question – how best to acquire and maximise profits? However, it also asks a second: What is the value of business beyond maximising profits for the traditional stake-holders – owners, workers and stockholders? Thirdly, what are the impacts – the consequences or effects – of acquiring those profits to the communities in which the business operates?

Principle-centred business asks about the ethics and morality of economics, about being accountable, about having a standard beyond mere profits by which business can and will be measured, judged and evaluated. Economics may be a benign science, but its historic effects have the power to lift up or bury millions.

Principles must be valued in business right along with profits.

Do we consider and attempt to measure the benefits that our goods and services contribute to the common good, social justice and environmental sustainability? The following quote from Paul Hawken puts these notions in even sharper perspective for both green and non-green businesses alike: "Even if every company on the planet were to adhere to the standards of the best socially and environmentally responsible companies, the world would still continue toward environmental degradation."[1]

There is no common agreement on what is/is not principled business or leadership. No doubt almost every businessperson considers that he conduct a principle centred business. Yet, there is no common agreement on what are/are not socially and environmentally responsible business values. Nor is there agreement on whose ethics/values are best, or how large profits must become before they are considered unethical. And, even if we could all agree on these concerns, there would be wide diversity of opinion regarding how the principles and values would actually be best carried out.

Ben and Jerry's Ice Cream has established two audits for themselves to measure business success: the traditional financial audit and the new business paradigm, a social audit. The social audit attempts to measure the impact of the business on the quality of the community and the people who live in that community. Examples: Ben and Jerry's has donated 7.5 per cent of its pre-tax earnings to non-profit organisations, while most corporations give less than 1 per cent of their pre-tax earnings to charity. "They deliberately support family farmers by paying more than the government recommends for milk; they use their packaging to advise value-oriented issues pertaining to peace and the environment. They consciously contribute to defending the rain forest by purchasing Brazil nuts from people in the rainforests and calling their product "Rainforest Crunch" in order to raise consciousness about the rainforest.[2]

A further and deeper inquiry into accountability of concern and interest to the career professional and job seeker, is whether principle centred business creates good work? The critic will quickly and rightly ask: who defines the nature of good work? Isn't the word "good" in good work relegated to completely subjective understanding? Can we determine objective criteria to which all can agree? While such clarity is difficult at best, and impossible absolutely, to strive in that direction is nonetheless a task well worth pursuing for the sake of this and future generations. This is said because even after the widely reported triumph of democracy and capitalism on the world scene in recent years, all is not well.

"In a random nationwide survey of children ages 10-13, 47 per cent believe they will be unhappy in the future, 45 per cent fear physical or sexual abuse, 50 per cent fear being kidnapped, and 51 per cent believe they may die prematurely." "Reported child abuse has increased 400 per cent in 25 years to 420 per 10,000 people. That's us good-hearted, let's-save-the-world, make love-not-war baby boomers beating up on our littlest kids while our older kids, are beating up on our grand-children." (Michael Phillips, in Whitmyer (ed.))[3]

According to Melissa Everett the following items are offered as criteria for defining and measuring good work, and thereby principle-centred business. Good work:

1. Enhances the worker through workplace opportunities that encourage creativity coupled with some measure of worker control in jobs that are inherently interested in producing something of lasting value.

2. Serves and supports other people in their lives and good work.
3. Causes as little harm to others and the environment as possible.[4]

Jobs are paced by market share, competition and micro-processor chip speed and not by the need for balance between work and leisure, or work and family, not by the natural cycles of day and night, or the seasons.

Computers are indifferent to the word balance. However, if we are to find balance, if we are to remain healthy in an unhealthy age, we, the workers, users and creators of computers and their applications, must take more responsibility for the effects or consequences to society of the use of new computer technologies. Good work serves, supports, brings joy and humour, comforts, nurtures, heals all who are touched by our performed tasks. As E.F. Schumacher noted, good work "ennobles the product as it ennobles the producer".

Good work nurtures our spirit as we nurture others' spirits. Good work focusses on creating opportunities in the form of jobs, careers and industries devoted to community well-being. Good work does not try to maximise the sale of goods and services solely for the sake of profit, stockholders, consumption or the satisfaction of advertising stimulated wants and desires over essentials and needs.

Evolving towards an economy primarily based on good work will witness the demise of some jobs and industries and the growth of others. This is the nature of any economic change. It is time to invest our work energy and money in businesses trying to incorporate these three criteria of good work rather than in businesses focussed almost exclusively on market share.

Good work does not eliminate the need for consumption and material acquisition as traditional economists fear. Good work merely alters the levels and kinds of consumption, seriously considers the impact of the production of particular goods and services on the community and seeks that the impact is as sustainable as possible – both economically and environmentally.

Principle-centred business factors in social, economic and environmental impacts as part of the increasing costs of doing business in any community or country almost regardless of local, state or federal compliance and regulation.

Finally, most jobs fail criterion three. Even though our society is making inroads in reducing waste and being more environmentally sensitive, the inevitable result of an increasing population and consumption of non-renewable resources is environmental degradation, resource depletion, a reduction in the quality of life and the increasing cost of almost everything, including stress induced mental and physical maladies of increasingly exotic kinds and complexity.

The following rules of thumb, which Goodpaster[5] referred to as "moral common sense", are significant here:

1. Avoid harming others,
2. Respect the rights of others,
3. Do not lie or cheat,
4. Keep promises and contracts,
5. Obey the law,
6. Prevent harm to others,
7. Help those in need,
8. Be fair, and
9. Reinforce these imperatives in others.

At first glance, these "commandments" are so convincing that further comment seems superfluous. When examined more closely, however, the picture is not so simple.

1. Avoid Harming Others

As said before, there is no need for a special ethics for the pharmaceutical industry. However, there are some important structural differences between the pharmaceutical industry and others. Drugs are not commodities in the sense of other consumer or investment goods. They are used because people are sick or in pain, or because they have physical or mental disorders, or because they are dying. "Consumer sovereignty", the freedom to choose or refuse a product, is limited in this industry's market. The resulting ethical challenge for the pharmaceutical industry, therefore, is pronounced.

Similarly, the pharmaceutical industry's assessments of drug safety and risk/benefit evaluations have particularly fateful properties: If the company's specialists or managers err, they err not just for themselves and their company, they err for the sick people who are at their mercy. Particularly obnoxious are double standards in safety for production or products, product information (indications, warnings on side-effects), product quality and everything else which is significant for the health or even the maintenance of human life.

2. Respect the Rights of Others

A great deal of the responsibility for the global environmental equilibrium rests with a small rich minority of about 15 per cent of the world's population. Their alarming ability to consume resources and create waste is responsible for about 80 per cent of the global environmental problems, including the potential greenhouse effect and the depletion of the ozone layer (*World Resources,* 1994-95). Per capita emissions of carbon dioxide and other greenhouse gases of Americans, Germans or Singaporeans is about ten-twenty times higher than those of the Indians and the Chinese, and about a hundred times higher than those of the people in Bangladesh. The same picture arises if we look at the per capita consumption of non-renewable resources. Clearly, the 10-15 per cent "rich" people – and among them, you and me – live unsustainable lifestyles when it comes to energy consumption, consumption of non-renewable resources, water consumption and pollution. Major ecological systems would probably have already collapsed, if all human beings lived the same lifestyle.

3. Do Not Lie or Cheat

The "three dogs theory" may be helpful to illustrate how one can easily fall into one's own trap: A man rings your door bell and complains that your dog has bitten him. Your first answer according to the theory is: "I do not have a dog!" That is the moment when your dog comes running around the house, barking loudly. You now refer to the "second dog theory" and say: "I do have a dog, but it does not bite." That is unfortunately the moment where your dog bites the man again. You then have to refer to your third and last dog theory: "I do have a dog, it does bite once in a while – but it does not hurt!" Your credibility, of course, fades away with every theoretical reorientation, as you are clearly only admitting what has already been proven. Furthermore, a "supposition gap" arises: Even after you have said everything you know, everyone still keeps waiting for the "fourth dog theory".

4. Keep Promises and Contracts

This commandment can be viewed from the perspective of the employee, but also from the other perspective, that of the corporation. An example could be the employees' working ethos: To paraphrase a quote from the late John F. Kennedy, one might suggest: "Don't ask what your company can do for you, but what you can do for your company." Solidarity means the morally qualified, essential and active dependence of the individual on the community and vice versa.

5. Obey the Law

Imagine you are travelling in a poor country in sub-Saharan Africa, or Southeast Asia or Latin America. And imagine further, you become seriously ill. And imagine further still, that you are very lucky – you find a well-trained physician who can diagnose your illness and knows how to treat it. If he gives you a prescription, it is highly probable that you do not know anything about the substances prescribed, unless you are yourself a physician or a pharmacist. But you recognise the name or the logo of the manufacturer, and if you can tie the name or the logo to a well-known, reputed pharmaceutical manufacturer, almost certainly you will feel relieved. You will expect that the worst will soon be over and you will be on your way to recovery.

6. Prevent Harm to Others

The safety of application of pesticides is a matter of widespread concern. Particularly in countries where illiteracy and other social conditions of poverty are pronounced, there is considerable worry about their public health impact (Geneva, 1990). And yet, safely and effectively used, pesticides can reduce losses due to insects, diseases and weeds, thus increasing income for the farmer and output of food for the nations concerned (Gunn & Stevens, 1976).

How far does the ethical responsibility of a specific agrochemical corporation reach? An individual corporation can certainly not run literacy and training courses for hundreds of thousands of people working in the rural areas of the developing world. It is certain that a company's ethical responsibility goes further than only selling its products to the next wholesale agent. Hence, more ought to be done, but how much more? The answer to that question depends very much on the specific social, economic and political framework of a specific country - and on the economic feasibility for the company concerned. Cooperation with the state extension services and manufacturers' associations is almost always part of an appropriate answer.

7. Help Those in Need

In our understanding of the social division of labour, it is not a primary function of business enterprises to become involved in charitable activities. As far as this is concerned, we firmly believe in subsidiarity and are convinced that global human development needs in the first place good governance and equitable economic relationships worldwide. Nevertheless, we are pleading for every social institution to do what it can from a humanitarian point of view. Ciba has been involved for years in numerous projects for people living in poverty through the Novartis Foundation for Sustainable Development (Novartis Foundation).

8. Be Fair

Here again, the application of the golden rule is an important point. It opens a variety of reflections, for example with regard to one's attitude towards colleagues on the same hierarchical level (key word: mobbing) and with regards to those who have lower ranks in the company (key words: respect, freedom, dignity).

9. Reinforce these Imperatives in Others

How can a corporation reinforce its moral imperatives in others? Should it have the courage to assume leadership responsibilities in ethically relevant questions – or should it seek conformity with convention as often happens in practice? Ethical guidelines of business associations are often the lowest common denominator and mostly fall short of what an individual corporation would be prepared to do with regard to higher ethical business standards.

The dilemma that arises when individual corporations obviously impair the image of the entire industry must also be considered here: Should one stay quiet and thus become a silent accomplice, or should one take the problem up and run the risk of being accused of washing one's dirty clothes in public?

In practice, it happens again and again that types of behaviour occur in a corporation which the corporate codes of conduct in force would forbid. Pitt and Groskaufmanis (1990) have developed criteria which can increase the practical effectiveness of internal codes of conduct.

Criteria for the formulation of corporate codes of conduct:

1. The principles of the code must be tailored to the specific corporate culture; merely taking over any general code is not enough.
2. The code of conduct addresses those activities of the corporation which are particularly sensitive or which concern the greatest vulnerability (legal, socio-political, and other such activities).
3. Corporate codes of conduct have to be pragmatic, i.e., they must reflect the circumstances of the corporation and should only set standards which can reasonably be expected to be followed.

Criteria for the implementation of corporate codes of conduct:

1. Firstly, a communication programme must ensure that all persons affected by the code of conduct actually know and understand it. It is not enough merely to distribute it, the content should be explained and someone made available to answer questions whenever the need arises.
2. There should be at least one person who may be approached in confidence (ombudsperson).
3. Employees should certify in writing that they have read, understood and will comply with the code of conduct in their work.

Criteria for the enforcement of corporate codes of conduct:

1. Working with codes of conduct only makes sense if the managers concerned are accountable for its objectives.
2. Audit committees, ombudspersons, a hotline or other means should ensure that employees can have their concerns taken up by the appropriate office.
3. Violations of the code of conduct must be investigated and resolved. The message should be clear and leave employees in no doubt: Violation of the code leads to penalties, including dismissal, and that irrespective of whether the violation had positive or detrimental consequences for the corporation.

Some examples of good work or, in other words, corporate values, maintained and carried by world-famous companies are summarised below, as beckoning examples:

General Electric (GE)

Respecting always the three traditions of GE...

Unyielding integrity, commitment to performance and thirst for change and:

Passion for our customers: Measuring our success by that of our customers...always driven by Six Sigma quality and a spirit of innovation,

Meritocracy: Creating opportunities for the best people from around the world to grow and live their dreams,

Growth driven, globally oriented: Growing our people, markets and businesses around the world,

Every person, every idea counts: Respecting the individual and valuing the contributions of each employee,

Playing offence: Using the advantages of size to take risks and try new things... never allowing size to be a disadvantage,

Embracing speed and excellence: Using the benefits of a digital age to accelerate our success and build a faster and smarter GE, and

Living the hallmarks of GE leadership:

Passion for learning and sharing ideas,

Committed to delivering results in every environment,

Ability to energise and inspire global, diverse teams, and

Connected to workplace, customers and communities... in touch with the world.

Ethics at Texas Instruments (TI)

More than 60 years ago, TI employees placed their personal imprint on the ethics of the company. They chose to conduct themselves to the highest standards of personal integrity, and they demanded the same of others. Today those principles and values still permeate all of TI's actions and decisions.

As TI grew, management recognised a need to formalise and communicate company standards. In 1961, TI published its first written code of ethics, a booklet titled, *Ethics in the Business of TI*. Though it has been revised several times to reflect changes in the business environment, the basic message contained in that first booklet has never changed, nor has TI's emphasis on maintaining a track record of ethics and integrity.

About 10 years ago, an increasing number of difficult issues, challenges and close calls in modern business were recognised, but clear choices of action did not always exist. Employees and their business associates needed to better understand TI's expectations and where they could go for help if they had a question or a concern. TI believes maintaining the highest ethical standards requires a partnership between employees and employers. The employer proactively supports employees by communicating values and giving individual guidance, while empowered employees participate actively in problem-solving. In 1987, TI decided to actively support employees by establishing a TI Ethics Office and appointing a TI Ethics Director.

The TI Ethics Office has three primary functions:

1. To ensure that business policies and practices continue to be aligned with ethical principles,
2. To clearly communicate ethical expectations, and
3. To provide multiple channels for feedback through which people can ask questions, voice concerns and seek solutions to ethical issues.

A reputation and track record for ethics and integrity is vital for establishing the trust that is the basis for all successful business relationships. All people associated with TI – employees, customers, suppliers, governments and communities – need to understand and appreciate the importance of these principles.

TI has strong documented requirements for ethical business practices:

1. TI Standard Policies and Procedures,
2. The TI Commitment, and
3. *The Values and Ethics of TI* booklet.

The direction is clear and the message is firmly and credibly supported by the highest levels of management and by the board of directors.

Ethics in the Global Market at TI

For many companies, increased competition, stricter government controls and emerging global markets have raised ethical questions that they were unprepared to deal with earlies.

"Ethical questions face business people every day, especially when a company is involved with worldwide markets," said Carl Skooglund, former vice-president and director of ethics, Texas Instruments. "Finding the right answer isn't often easy – one has to balance local customs and laws with US laws."

As an international company with more than 44,500 employees operating in more than 25 countries, TI is global in scope and culture with a time-honoured tradition of conducting business in an ethical and legal manner. But that is an increasingly difficult challenge fuelled by the changing times, relationships and situations facing companies today.

TI's global vision is World Leadership in Digital Solutions for the Networked Society. The company is competing to win at a global level – entering into strategic partnerships, alliances and joint ventures in every corner of the globe. The success of these relationships depends greatly upon the company's representatives understanding the ethical standards and expectations of others. Consider these examples of cultural differences from the Ethics Office files:

1. In the US, telephone helplines or "hotlines", as some companies refer to them, are considered a normal part of business. In some parts of the world, however, hotlines may be greatly mistrusted or even viewed as personally offensive and dangerous,
2. US companies and US citizens are subject to certain US laws wherever they are. Other countries also have a global reach, and
3. Workers in some parts of the world consider the concept of ethics to be very personal and they may not fully understand that it is also a global or companywide issue to be discussed or even questioned. In many places, the contract negotiation process can be very long and drawn out – and somewhat informal. That's very frustrating for most US companies unless they have a good understanding of

what's going on. There may be very good intentions on all frouts, but unless everyone clearly understands the process, it may seem that something unethical is happening.

"These types of situations are trying in the best of times. But today, many organisations and people are under enormous pressure to succeed in a very competitive and challenging global economy. Companies are reducing or eliminating layers of management that made the decisions that they are now expecting those on the firing line to make. We are in a world where the ability to communicate rapidly has exploded. It has created enormous opportunities as well as risks. Legal complexities have increased to the point that people simply don't know. In fact, they can't know," said Skooglund

"Our relationships with other companies are changing through alliances, partnerships and joint ventures to the point that at different times, we may be dealing with other companies as customers, suppliers or competitors. Yet, we still expect employees to recognise and respect those differences and the legal risks they present," he said.

The challenge in this dynamic environment, with its close calls and uncertainties, according to Skooglund, "is to provide tools to our employees so that they can make tough, quick decisions on the fly, on the firing line. And make them correctly. There are two elements to making decisions and taking action on behalf of an organisation: 1. a clear understanding of the organisation's values, principles and ethical expectations, and 2. sound personal judgement and appropriate choices."

To meet these challenges, TI has adopted a three-level approach to ethical integrity on a global level. The first level simply asks: Are we complying with all legal requirements on a local level?

The next level asks: Are there business practices or requirements at the local level which impact how we interact with co-workers in other parts of the world? A growing number of local regulations – rigid environmental regulations in some parts of Europe, for example – have a significant effect on products that we ship to and from those countries.

The third level is: Do some of our practices need to be adapted based on the local laws and customers of a specific locale? What we think is perfectly proper in one country may not migrate well to another. On what basis do we define our universal standards that apply to TI employees everywhere?

For example, Skooglund explained: "TI generally follows conservative rules covering the giving and receiving of gifts. However, what we consider to be an excessive gift in the US may differ from what local customs dictate in other parts of the world. We used to define gift limits in terms of US dollars, but this is impractical when dealing internationally. Instead, we emphasise following the directive that gift-giving should not be used in a way that exerts undue pressure to win business or implies a *quid pro quo*.

"In today's environment, there is no way that a rule book or a library of policies are going to guide those actions. They must be guided by a shared understanding of basic values and principles of integrity. And they must be supported by resources that will help people to recognise when the warning lights should come on and to know where they can seek expert advice quickly. TI's reputation is completely in our hands, to be enhanced or damaged by the nature of our actions," he concluded.

3M's Vision and Strategy

3M's environmental, health and safety policies are directly linked to 3M's four fundamental corporate values:

1. Respecting our social and physical environment,
2. Satisfying customers with superior quality and value,
3. Providing an attractive return for investors and
4. Being a company that employees can be proud of.

3M's Vision

3M's vision is to contribute to society's move to sustainable development. To 3M, sustainable development means meeting the needs of customers today, while respecting the ability of future generations to meet their needs.

3M's process for moving toward sustainability is called eco-efficiency – first defined by the World Business Council for Sustainable Development. This means producing more products and services with fewer resources and less environmental, health and safety impact.

3M Strategies for Continuous Improvement

The company's participation in sustainability is advanced by the 3M environmental management system (EMS), which requires continuous improvement through three main strategies.

Strategy One

Continue improving its compliance assurance systems to meet and exceed government and 3M standards.

Strategy Two

Maintain emphasis on life cycle management, considering environmental, health and safety opportunities and issues for all stages of a product's life-cycle – from development and manufacturing through customer use and final disposal.

Strategy Three

Meet 3M's aggressive goals for environmental, health and safety impact and move as close to zero as possible for environmental releases, injuries and illnesses.

General Motors (GM)

GM has defined six core values for the conduct of its business:

1. Continuous improvement,
2. Customer enthusiasm,
3. Innovation,
4. Integrity,
5. Teamwork, and
6. Individual respect and responsibility.

These values are the basis upon which all GM employees conduct their day-to-day business, and are the foundation of GM's guidelines for employee conduct, *Our Values and Guidelines for Employee Conduct.* These guidelines, which demonstrate GM's commitment to integrity, include personal integrity, integrity in the workplace, integrity in the marketplace and integrity in society and its communities.

In May 1999, GM announced its support of the Global Sullivan Principles of Social Responsibility (See: Appendix I) as being consistent with GM's internal policies and principles, including its *Winning with Integrity* guidelines. The Global Sullivan Principles, which were developed by the Reverend Leon H. Sullivan and have their roots in the 1977 Sullivan Principles for South Africa, provide guidance to companies across the globe regarding core issues such as human rights, worker rights, the environment, community relations, supplier relations and fair competition.

Problems in the Present System

Our present society has fundamental structural and institutional problems that we must recognise and manage to resolve. We must change the basic operating principles and values of the structures of our society if we are to move in a more moral, ethical and spiritual direction. For instance, because the economic system only values what is marketed or traded, everything else is considered an externality of no importance to economic analysis. A fundamental problem with economics is that it maintains inadequate accounts. Paying attention only to what has monetary value, economic analysis misses much of what is happening in society. It is like trying to take care of an automobile only by keeping the tank filled and ignoring everything else necessary to keep it running safely. Moreover, society also follows the wrong economic guidelines. Take a measure like gross domestic product. GDP is widely equated with prosperity: higher GDP means greater prosperity. However, GDP also grows because more people are suffering from the health effects of pollution; it grows if more automobile accidents occur requiring repairs, replacements and medical treatment. So GDP is no accurate measure of prosperity and ought not to be used to measure it. The use of monetary measures is similarly inadequate. Too often people say "more money equals prosperity." But you cannot eat money. If food runs out, money has no value at all. Neither money nor profit can measure human happiness and well-being.

Another problem is the importance that economists attach to growth. To them, growth is needed for success: a company has to grow, the economy must expand. But the planet is a limited system, and sooner or later we are going to reach its environmental limits. Economics also ignores social limits, not to mention the optimal scales of functionality. Each organism has a particular optimal size. Corporations that get too big either must break down into profit centres or go out of business. Sometimes they do, or are bought out and broken up into more manageable elements. Certain optimal scales exist for any system, but economics is not very scale-sensitive. It strives for growth regardless of its impact on the overall system.

The drive for increased productivity is another issue in which the logic of individual decisions has a perverse collective impact on society. Raising productivity is an economic imperative. A company must raise its productivity and reduce its labour costs to increase its profitability. Yet this ignores the fact that employees are also consumers. If the number of people earning wages declines, there are that many fewer consumers to buy products and services. It is a case of sawing off the branch you are sitting on. To benefit the economy in a real sense, why not seek to make everybody a consumer by ensuring total employment. Instead, decision-making in the corporate system moves in the opposite direction. This is encouraged by another structural problem in Western economies: the privatisation of employment and the socialisation of unemployment. In other words, companies reduce their labour costs in the short term by transferring to the government the cost of maintaining the redundant workers. Such a short-sighted system ignores the importance of work as a contribution to society and a spiritual obligation.

Problems with globalisation generate increasing controversy. Globalisation has freed the movement of capital, and the World Trade Organisation has a mandate to globalise the movement of goods and services. But nobody wants to talk about the third essential dimension of globalisation, the free movement of people. Such free movement would be a great global equalizer, breaking down the disparities between countries rich and poor. If a country did not want the masses of the poor pouring across its borders, it would pay for them to stay at home. Since few of us like to leave home if we can avoid it, this would become a powerful force for redistributing resources more justly. It would also help to bring populations back in balance with environmental resources. Where there are more resources, people could come and develop them. Where there are not enough, people could move away. If through climate change the grain basket of the American Middle West turned into a desert and Siberia became fertile, should we wait for several new generations of Russians to grow up to populate Siberia with farmers, or do we allow experienced American grain farmers to move there? It will be a challenge to resolve such problems of shifts in carrying capacity around the world, but they are going to become an increasing part of the dynamics in the years ahead.

Then, of course, the economic system ignores the poor. Since they are not consumers, the poor are excluded or forgotten. Their presence illustrates a series of fundamental failures in present mechanisms for redistributing wealth within society. Any developed society considers extremes of wealth and poverty to be unacceptable. The poor cannot be left to die while the rich walk over their bodies, of course; so at least some effort is made to put the poor out of sight in some way. There is, however, a greater moral principle that requires some level of wealth sharing, and taxation systems are designed to do that. Yet, it is possible to escape taxation. With globalisation, wealth creation is increasingly reported not in the countries with strong tax systems, but in the Cayman Islands, Vanuatu and other so-called tax havens. Such avoidance of taxation is logical within a system in which the first priority is to maximise profit. Multi-nationals increasingly shift their real wealth creation out of places where taxation is heavy, escaping the mechanisms that allow restoration of the social balance. One of the most fundamental crises with globalisation today is the breakdown of the mechanisms for redistributing wealth.

Nor does the present economic system assign a meaningful priority to the needs of the poor. Where there is no potential income, there is no market and, therefore, no business interest. As a result, there is little incentive, in terms of the profit motive, in developing medicines to combat the diseases of the poor who cannot afford to buy them. There are many choices between elaborate technologies that can sell for a high price and those technologies that people can do for themselves without expensive inputs. Most business effort goes into products that yield profits. No mechanism encourages people to use technology they can apply themselves because there is no market for it. The profit motive, not the well-being of people or the overall benefit to humanity, pushes development towards high technology.

With respect to environmental sustainability, the economic system falls to deal effectively with most environmental problems. It works at the wrong scales in time and space. The economic system is very short term, while most environmental problems are long term, planetary, and occur on a very large scale. Businesses only deal with some small fragments of such problems. No mechanism puts together individual forms of corporate behaviour to enable us to look at the larger picture. The result is a fundamental miss-match when it comes to dealing with such large-scale problems as carbon-dioxide accumulation, the ozone hole, persistent organic pollutants, soil and water management, and the like. Too often, the economic system falls to come to grips with the essential issues because it tries to deal with them at the wrong scales in space and time.

Another area of growing concern involves intellectual property. In economic terms, we are witnessing a new "privatisation" of "the commons." Businesses are exploring ways to make money by buying (or privatising) information (the commons) that it can then sell at a profit. Unlike most products, however, the more information is shared, the greater its value to society. Information on good soil management, for example, can be sold as a product only to farmers who can afford it, leaving other farmers to continue destructive agricultural practices. Obviously, there would be greater benefit by making such information available to all who can use it. This brings us to a point where two fundamental value systems collide.

In agriculture, two systems operate simultaneously: on one side is the Consultative Group of International Agricultural Research institutions; on the other are the great multinational agribusiness firms. The research institutes created the Green Revolution over many years with funds from the Rockefeller Foundation, the World Bank and other institutional sources. The institutes maintain gene banks for various crops, sharing the genetic resources freely around the world; they breed new crops adapted to the great variety of conditions that exist in the world. As the results of the Green Revolution show, this system of sharing information works very effectively, boosting nutrition and reducing hunger globally. Contrast that record with that of agribusiness companies that are buying up and patenting genetic resources to produce crops that will be the more profitable because the companies sell not only the seeds, but the herbicides, pesticides and fertilizers needed to coax maximum output from the seeds. They can sell the resulting "one-size-fits-all" package to farmers around the world, minimising costs and maximising profits. While uniform varieties can work under ideal conditions, they are vulnerable to new or more resistant diseases. One year, an epidemic suddenly swept through the corn in the American Middle West because the same hybrid seeds had been sown everywhere. This approach goes in the wrong direction. Though it may increase short-term profits for the agribusiness firms involved, it narrows the' genetic base of our major food crops and, therefore, is ecologically unsustainable. These two systems operate simultaneously with two totally different approaches to intellectual property. One privatises it in order to reap the greatest profit for the owning corporation; the other makes the information available for the good of all humanity. This results in serious conflicts in terms of moral values, ethical principles, and operating practices - conflicts that the business community needs to think hard about.

The questions posed by these problems are fundamentally ethical: How do we foster a new moral, ethical and spiritual foundation in business? How do we establish new ground rules for business to help it contribute to a more sustainable society? How can we create a broader legal and institutional framework in which business can work to overcome the problems of fragmentation of responsibility and of inadequate or absent moral and ethical accountability? The root of the problem lies in the way in which economic institutions are structured. We need to explore how we can maintain the vitality of corporate structures and their ability to evolve quickly, but within a framework built around ethical, moral and spiritual values that will help the system work effectively for society as a whole.

New Values for Business

Let us examine for a moment the necessary new values and operating principles that would underlie a more sustainable society. On the individual level, they are readily apparent: if we want to improve human relationships we need more love, more altruism. We need a sense of justice, a willingness to share wealth and make sacrifices. We need a sense of solidarity with the human race, a sense of serving all humanity. We need a more spiritually oriented work ethic, a sense of moderation and contentment with fewer material goods. If we want to achieve sustainability, if we want to share resources effectively around the world and allow everybody to develop so that wealth is open to all, we must change our values with respect to material things and adopt a willingness to see wealth redistributed in order to reduce the dangerous extremes of wealth and poverty. We must become trustworthy and more respectful of creation and all that surrounds us. At the individual level, the more we can strengthen those values in each of us, the more we shall be equipped with the right kind of operating principles to build a sustainable society.

The same is true institutionally, since these same values can be applied to business. We can, at the business level, create a sense of service to society, recognise that business does not exist Just to make money, but also to serve society. We can build the value of service into business. Business systems can easily adapt to a service orientation, but only if the goal broadens beyond profit seeking. If that is done, the driving force behind business becomes much more constructive than it is now.

The principle of justice also has applications in business. These applications include sharing profits with all the corporation's workers and involving them in decision making. Justice can apply also to such prosaic things as interest rates. Islam forbade usury, and in early Christianity charging interest was prohibited. That is why Jews, not so restricted by their faith, could make the money that nobody else was allowed to make.

Business also needs to pay more attention to the sustainable management of natural resources. These should be considered as capital accounts. As with managing any other capital account, net losses are to be avoided. Business activity should produce no net loss for any of its capital accounts, be they economic accounts, human accounts or resource accounts. In the same way, businesses should avoid any net transfer of costs, or capital losses, to future generations or other parts of the world. Each generation's accounts should ultimately balance. This, of course, requires new accounting systems to allow us to calculate these various accounts, and that remains a big, challenge.

Economic activity also must respect the limits of Earth's life-support systems and ecological processes. Because many of those processes are planetary, respecting them will require building new global institutions for managing them at that level. This institution building is another major challenge before us.

Let us consider the market mechanism as an example of how values influence the economic system. Markets are based on competition, and all too often on some form of manipulation. A used car salesman may, for example, hide the fact that a vehicle he seeks to sell at the highest possible price has been involved in an accident that produced damage not visible to the potential buyer. Moreover, in sectors in which there are few competitors, price-fixing may be arranged to increase revenues for each participant in the scheme. Absent ethical values, or effective outside regulation, markets may seem more competitive than they actually are, just as the damaged car may appear better than it really is. But markets work best if they operate on principles of truthfulness and open consultation. Market theory is based on perfect information, but available information is rarely perfect. Prices would be set more fairly, for example, if the seller openly shared the real cost of production and the buyer fairly portrayed his or her need for the product. Consultation fosters the setting of a price that fairly balances the seller's cost and the buyer's need in terms of willingness to pay. Just so, the market would work more effectively if it were infused with a spirit of collaboration and consultation rather than, as at present, with a competitive spirit seeking to see which sides can best the others. In short, it is not so much the mechanics of the economic system that are wrong, but the values that underlie it. They need to be replaced or adjusted if we are to develop more sustainable mechanisms in society.

Towards a More Sustainable Society

We need to find ways to make decisions within a planetary perspective, since we are dealing with a global system. Planet

Earth is one country and, therefore, we need to be able to integrate decision-making up and down the various component levels – international, national, regional, local. We must also redistribute responsibility among these various levels. There has been too much centralisation at the level of national governments and multinational corporations. Many systems work better when they devolve responsibilities to smaller units. This may mean investing responsibility in communities or among resource-users at the local level, or devolving it to smaller units within a business, whether as profit centres or quality-control programs. So we must rethink our institutional arrangements and devise ways of applying the principle of what the European Union calls "subsidiarity" in redesigning the system. This applies equally within business and generally within society.

Some global structures already exist, of course, in the form of multinational businesses and such international bodies as the World Trade Organisation (WTO). The WTO has teeth and can impose sanctions if necessary in resolving trade disputes between its member nations. But we lack balance globally across the different sectors: there is no WTO of the environment, for example, only a few general principles. Because we lack balance in our global institutions, we witness stresses and strains every time the WTO tries to meet.

Businesses need fairness operating on a global basis. They have difficulty dealing with differing regulations, corrupt systems, and so forth. It is, therefore, in the interest of business to strengthen global mechanisms and establish a level playing field. To achieve that, it would be reasonable for businesses to pay taxes, assuming, of course, that the taxes were applied fairly. As business becomes more enlightened, it will become a leading force to establish effective global institutions, since these institutions will be good for business. Governments hold back for fear of losing power and eroding national sovereignty. So leadership has to come from elsewhere. Businesses are, in many ways, well placed to lead the effort to build the structures all of us need to make this system operate more effectively on a global basis.

We also need to look at all the issues of social welfare and redistribution of wealth. New information technologies make intolerable the kinds of inequities and injustices that have survived for generations because of ignorance. When the poor can see via satellite television how the rich live (and often it is how the rich live as portrayed by Hollywood), they observe extreme differences between rich and poor. Is it any wonder, really, that people fly airplanes into buildings and blow themselves up as "martyrs" because what they witness through today's information technology is simply no longer tolerable? In that sense, technology is driving us towards greater social justice. What is lacking are the mechanisms to implement and apply social justice on a global level.

We need, too, to find ways to balance all the accounts not only within corporations and within nations, but also globally. And these accounts, whether they be social accounts or environmental accounts, are seriously out of balance. Here we face an enormous challenge, one that we can overcome through voluntary acts of consultative will or else we will be forced to respond to the challenge because of crises and catastrophe. At this point we seem to be more beset by crises and catastrophe than benefiting from voluntary will. But the potential is there. And business can provide the leadership needed to push society into a more constructive direction. We need to get affluent Western society to move away from ultra-materialism and excessive consumerism, and, in doing so, simplify its life-style and increase its efficiency. Through greater simplicity in our lives and improved efficiency, we can maintain a similar quality of life while reducing by a factor of ten our consumption of energy and resources. Studies done in Europe show this to be technically possible. So one of the challenges for business is to find ways to raise efficiency, reduce use of materials, increase production of services, and support recycling processes. By doing so, we can achieve these technically challenging but attainable goals.

However, we must also look at another dimension, that of empowering the poor. We must learn how to involve poor people directly in their own development, without imposing on them our own view of development. We must organise the process so people can guide their own development, set their own values, and decide their own priorities for using resources. And we must build more organic societies, evolving themselves from the ground up and adapted to the wide variety of situations around the world.

One tool for accomplishing this derives from the principle of the independent investigation of truth: it is the recognition that science is for everyone. Once we all become accustomed to thinking scientifically and in terms of process, we will understand how to monitor the environment, observe the changes taking place, and adjust our behaviour accordingly. This extends the principle of subsidiarity to science, as everybody becomes a scientific manager, everybody becomes part of the new operating systems, and we become able to build a more sustainable society. This is a way, too, of combining science and religion, of combining ethical or spiritual considerations with the principles of science and technology. By doing so we can create a multi-level system in which, at each level, these processes operate together. The result will be a new kind of self-generating civilisation, one that is ever-advancing, bringing prosperity to all the world's population.

The business community has a key role in helping us view life from a systems perspective, a perspective which is essential as we move towards a more sustainable society. We shall achieve that by getting the basic working rules right and then letting the system evolve. If our greatest challenge lies in the economic arena, it is because the present rules governing its operations are so at variance with society's real needs. As we build more sustainable businesses, we create more sustainable economies. And, we set in motion the processes necessary to achieve a more sustainable civilisation. That is our goal.

Here, an example of Global Compact will teach us some lessons for building corporate citizenship.[6]

The Compact is a voluntary initiative promoting responsible global corporate citizenship. It operates on a leadership model in that it aims to bring a critical mass of business leaders on board to build a sustainable movement. A company's CEO, endorsed by the company's board, must take the initiative to write to the Secretary-General stating the organisation's commitment to the Compact and its principles. Once this commitment is made, a company:

- Sets in motion changes to business operations so that the Global Compact and its principles become part of strategy, culture and day-to-day operations.
- Is expected to publicly advocate the Global Compact and its principles via communications vehicles such as press releases speeches etc.
- Is expected to publish in its annual financial report or similar document (e.g., sustainability report) a description of the ways in which it is supporting the Global Compact and all its principles.

For sustainability reports, the Global Compact encourages the use of the Global Reporting Initiative. In addition, it supports dialogue with companies by others engaged in the Compact. Special efforts are being made to reach out to small and medium-sized enterprises, including through UNIDO (United Nations Industrial Development Organization), the IOE (International Organization of Employers) member federations and international sectoral associations. The Global Compact office neither regulates nor monitors a company's submissions and initiatives. The Compact's website carries the names of the companies that have sent letters of support and provides links to relevant reports. Global Compact network partners facilitate implementation of the nine principles by submitting business case studies and examples and by offering training and tools. Participating companies also have the opportunity to contribute to a number of Global Compact activities at the global and local levels, through dialogue, learning and partnership projects.

Labour

Labour is part of both industry and civil society. It plays a role that is distinct from both business and other elements of civil society. That is why it is recognised in the Compacts a separate group. Internationally recognised Labour standards, including the fundamental rights that are part of the nine principles of the Compact, are developed in a tripartite process in which business and Labour play central roles. They are also heavily involved in the supervisory procedures of the ILO (International Labour Organization) to try to ensure that labour standards are implemented at the national level. The structures of the international trade union movement equip it to coherently participate in the Compact in a way that covers sector and sectoral engagement as well as general policy issues. Trade unions are representative organisations that bring to the table long traditions of internal democracy, transparency and accountability to members.

Civil Society Organisations

Civil society organisations (CSOs) add critical dimensions to the Compact's operations. They offer not just their competencies and substantive knowledge but their problem-solving capacity and practical reach. Also, they can help to provide checks and balances and lend credibility and social legitimacy to the initiative. These characteristics help entrench the Compact's principles in a broader social context. When participating in dialogue, CSOs add value to the processes of relationship building, information sharing, problem-solving and consensus building. As project partners, their practical reach and skills are often crucial to the design and implementation of initiatives that give practical meaning to the Compact's principles. These initiatives also help to maximise learning efforts associated with a company's Compact-related activities. Since dialogue involves multiple, diverse stakeholders, the Compact asks all participants to respect the common policy space that the Compact offers. This is done to ensure that dialogue remains constructive and produces meaningful outcomes. In fact, participants should be prepared to make a statement to this effect to the Global Compact office. In sum, four traits are essential to participate in the Compact's activities: the willingness to engage with all actors of society, the proven ability to make a substantive contribution, the ability to transcend a single-issue orientation, and the proof of a minimum level of transparency and accountability in matters such as membership and funding. Participating CSOs are certainly at liberty to pursue their own approaches outside the framework of the Compact.

Leadership

The leadership engagement mechanism represents a company's entry point and overall commitment to the Global Compact principles. As mentioned earlier, the goal is to create a critical mass of dedicated business leaders to sustain the movement. Initially, accompany intent on joining the Compact had to send in a letter of commitment from the CEO. The company also had to submit an example of its work in implementing the Global Compact principles. Now, this commitment should ideally be endorsed by the company board. In addition, to raise transparency and public accountability, companies are expected to issue a 'Communication on Progress' in their annual reports or other prominent public documents, such as sustainability reports which will be linked to the Global Compact website. For sustainability reports, companies are encouraged to use indicators such as those identified in the Guidelines of the Global Reporting Initiative (GRI). The requirement for an example is no longer mandatory.

Dialogue

Dialogue is central to the Compact. The overall objective of the Global Compact 'Policy Dialogues' is to create a platform that facilitates mutual understanding and joint efforts among business, labour and NGOs in solving key challenges of globalisation, working with governments and the UN. The objective is to both influence policy making and the behaviour of all stakeholders. The outcomes of dialogue fall into three categories. The upstream products are those that can engender changes in policy frameworks, encompassing both incentive structures and regulatory mechanisms. Downstream products can influence the actual behaviour of participants. Collective action is the third outcome. Through accumulated experience, the dialogue objectives for the past year have gained renewed clarity. The first overarching goal was to seek maximum practical application for products resulting from earlier dialogues. The second goal was to further professionalise and reinforce the capacity to organise and effectively conduct multi stakeholder dialogues. The following four specific objectives were set: First, efforts were to be directed at obtaining wide application by multiple stakeholders of dialogue products developed in 2001 and 2002. Second, the initiative to "grow sustainable businesses in least developed countries" was to be facilitated. Third, a new round of dialogues on specific issues was to be launched. Fourth, efforts were to be directed at refining the concept and methodology of dialogues to increase effectiveness of processes and outcomes.

Governance

As a voluntary corporate citizenship initiative, the Compact has maintained an open network structure, and conscious efforts have been made to eliminate bureaucratic controls. It utilises the power of transparency, dialogue and accountability to identify good practices and to find practical solutions to a range of problems and challenges. Willingness and ability to be part of the solution are the overriding criteria for engagement. As the UN Secretary-General's initiative, the Global Compact office in New York is at the heart of the network, together with five UN core agencies. Three of these are sometimes referred to as the "guardians of the principles". The OHCHR (Office of the High Commissioner for Human Rights), the ILO (International Labour Organization) and the UNEP (UN Environment Programme). UNIDO' s strength lies in dealing with small and medium-sized enterprises; the UNDP (UN Development

Programme) is the UN's global operational arm. Other UN agencies participate whenever necessary and appropriate. A number of safeguards have been developed to protect the integrity of the UN. Rules that govern the use of the UN logo are in place. Also, the Compact has created and follows a self-imposed rule of accepting funding only from governments or non-profit organisations. Appropriate measures will be taken if individual participants use their association with the Compact for purposes other than its stated goals or if their individual behaviour threatens the initiative's integrity. The Compact is not a substitute for effective regulation and action by governments. Rather, it is an opportunity for participants to exercise voluntary leadership in the spirit of enlightened self-interest. The Compact is intended to be an initiative that is complementary to government efforts and regulation. It helps establish the business case for doing the right thing. By setting examples within its own sphere of influence, it hopes to generate positive impulses that in turn can contribute towards governance and public policy responses that contribute to a more beneficial relationship between business and society. The Compact is not strategically positioned to compete with other voluntary initiatives. Instead, it seeks to build on complementarities and to reinforce initiatives that advance the goals of the Compact, assuming that, over time, content compatibility and convergence will lead to effective global norms that are unique in their universality and legitimacy. The Compact's Advisory Council is composed of personalities of outstanding accomplishment and expertise from business, labour, civil society and academia. The Council provides strategic advice to the Secretary-General.

Finally, the Compact principles can be agonizingly complex to execute. At its core, the Compact is nothing more than a moral compass. Its simplicity, then, resides in the crystal-like clarity that only a moral compass can give. Its complexity arises from precisely the same clarity, that at its core it is nothing less than a moral compass. The Compact principles suggest that multiple actors with often seemingly irreconcilable beliefs pull in concert towards a common vision. Actors should then agree on how to navigate the unclear boundaries between belief and bigotry, responsibility and accountability, interventions and interference. Players in the capitalist system would need to agree on where competition ends and where collective conscience begins. Many will remember the popular slogan used during the growth of the environmental movement: "We have met the enemy, and he is us." The time is now ripe for Compact actors to realise that they have met at least a part of the solution, and that it is them. The Compact's relevance will lie in the decision participants make to either build a sustainable society that offers opportunity to the world's citizens

The Ultimate Issue

The business community has a key role in helping us view life from a systems perspective, a perspective which is essential as we move towards a more sustainable society. We shall achieve that by getting the basic working rules right and then letting the system evolve. If our greatest challenge lies in the economic arena, it is because the present rules governing its operations are so at variance with society's real needs. As we build more sustainable businesses, we create more sustainable economies. And we set in motion the processes necessary to achieve a more sustainable civilisation. That is our prime goal to make the global citizens happy and prosperous.

Notes

1. *The Ecology of Commerce.*
2. Quoted from Matthew Fox in *The Reinvention of Work*, p. 320.
3. Adapted from an article in *Mindfulness and Meaningful Work*, Ed. by Claude Whitmyer, p. 111. The article was written by Michael Phillips.

4. Quoted from Melissa Everett's book, *Making a Living while Making a Difference*.
5. K.E. Goodpaster, *Ethics in Management*, Harvard Business School, Boston, 1984, p. 6.
6. Global Compact Website.

Appendix I

The Global Sullivan Principles of Social Responsibility, a code of conduct built on a vision of aspiration and inclusion, provides a framework to which socially responsible companies and organisations can align themselves. The principles are inclusive in that they embrace businesses' existing codes of conduct and work in conjunction with them. The aspiration of the principles is to have companies and organisations of all sizes, in widely disparate industries and cultures, working toward the common goals of human rights, social justice and economic opportunity. These principles are truly unique; they apply to all workers, in all industries, in all countries.

Reverend Leon H. Sullivan created the Global Sullivan Principles at the request of world and industry leaders, with inputs from a number of multinational corporations and business associations. Reverend Sullivan's vision was that of business working hand-in-hand with the community to advance social responsibility and the culture of peace. We urge companies large and small, as well as all types of business and non-profit organisations, governments and education providers, to endorse the principles and make Reverend Sullivan's vision a lasting reality.

Each endorser of the Global Sullivan Principles makes a commitment to work towards the aspiration that the principles represent, including the implementation of internal policies, procedures, training and reporting structures. Endorsing companies and organisations are asked to take part in an annual reporting process to document and share their experiences in bringing social responsibility to life. The reporting format has been designed to be flexible, transparent and easy to complete. All reports submitted will be made available on the Global Sullivan Principles website.

Reverend Sullivan's goal also included measures to support the efforts of those who have stepped forward to endorse the Global Sullivan Principles. The reports submitted annually by endorsers will be reviewed in order to highlight efforts of note. An annual meeting of endorsers will be convened to share the experiences, benefits and challenges of implementing the Global Sullivan Principles.

The Global Sullivan Principles are intended to be strong in aspiration, yet flexible and relevant to all types of industries and cultures. Comments and inputs are welcomed from our endorsers and other interested parties.

A company which endorses the Global Sullivan Principles will respect the law and, as a responsible member of society, will apply these principles with integrity consistent with the legitimate role of business. The company will develop and implement company policies, procedures, training and internal reporting structures to ensure commitment to these principles throughout their organisation. Members believe the application of these principles will achieve greater tolerance and better understanding among peoples, and advance the culture of peace.

Accordingly, members will:

1. Express their support for universal human rights and, particularly, those of their employees, the communities within which they operate, and parties with whom they do business,
2. Promote equal opportunity for their employees at all levels of the company with respect to issues such as colour, race, gender, age, ethnicity or religious beliefs, and operate without unacceptable worker treatment such as the exploitation of children, physical punishment, female abuse, involuntary servitude, or other forms of abuse,

3. Respect their employees' voluntary freedom of association,
4. Compensate their employees to enable them to meet at least their basic needs and provide the opportunity to improve their skill and capability in order to raise their social and economic opportunities,
5. Provide a safe and healthy workplace; protect human health and the environment; and promote sustainable development,
6. Promote fair competition, including respect for intellectual and other property rights, and not offer, pay or accept bribes,
7. Work with governments and communities in which they do business to improve the quality of life in those communities – their educational, cultural, economic and social well-being – and seek to provide training and opportunities for workers from disadvantaged backgrounds,
8. Promote the application of these principles by those with whom they do business, and
9. The company will be transparent in its implementation of these principles and provide information which demonstrates publicly their commitment to them.

Index